Nadia

Love x

Justine

The mymuybueno® Cookbook

⊚ Eat ⊚ Live ⊚ Learn

The mymuybueno® Cookbook

160 REFINED SUGAR-FREE RECIPES FOR EVERYDAY EATING IN YOUR BUSY LIFE

JUSTINE MURPHY

PHOTOGRAPHY BY
CLARE WINFIELD & PERNILLA DANIELSSON

me:ze
PUBLISHING

Photography © Clare Winfield
Cover, 2-3, 21, 28-35, 38-41, 45, 48-62, 67, 70-76, 81-161, 166-174, 179-211, 215-231, 234-250, 254-257, 261, 264-268, 273-275

Photography © Pernilla Danielsson
1, 5-17, 27, 36-37, 43, 46, 64-65, 69, 78-79, 162, 164-165,176-177, 212-213, 232-233, 252-253, 258-259, 262, 271, 276-288

First edition printed in 2020 in the UK.
ISBN: 978-1-910863-54-1

Author: Justine Murphy
Editor: Phil Turner
Editing: Katie Fisher and Vanessa Flaxman
Design: Paul Cocker and Brigita Butvila
Brand Design: mymuybueno
Art Direction: Justine Murphy
Food Styling: Jennifer Joyce
Prop Styling: Zoe Harrington
Hair and Make Up: Jam Deluxe
Printed in Great Britain by Bell and Bain Ltd, Glasgow

Published by Meze Publishing Limited
Unit 1b, 2 Kelham Square
Kelham Riverside
Sheffield S3 8SD
Web: www.mezepublishing.co.uk
Telephone: 0114 275 7709
Email: info@mezepublishing.co.uk

For my Granny, the most amazing woman I have had the privilege to know.

Paul, thank you for always believing in me and my mymuybueno vision.

My boys, Seth and Jacob, you complete me.

For anyone who has been through the hardest of times, to believe and
know that through hard work, passion and a dream,
anything is possible, this book is also for you.

CONTENTS

Introduction

This book is all about the power and importance of having good food in our lives. It is a book packed full of my favourite recipes that are healthy as well as delicious, easy to adapt and easy to master. But it's not only about the food itself; it's also about taking the time to enjoy it: cooking, breaking bread, feeding yourself and the people you love, and spending time in their company. It's about valuing the precious moments in our ever-busy lives, enhancing your day-to-day and focusing on building the lives that we deserve.

It was through good food, good people and cooking my way to happiness that I was able to heal my wounds and create the life that I always dreamt of

My journey through life has proven that no matter what it may bring, or what one's past may look like, it is possible to achieve anything. My past was filled with darkness and adversity, but it was through good food, good people and cooking my way to happiness that I was able to heal my wounds and create the life that I always dreamt of, and that I have worked so very hard to achieve. Through opening up and sharing my story I have realised how many people I am able to help, people who can find inspiration from a part of my journey and use it to start changing their own.

My company, mymuybueno, is all about good food and good people. It began as a vision for running my own business based on everything I had learnt, using all the confidence I had gained by overcoming adversity and forging a career for myself. It wasn't a small vision by any means; from the very beginning I knew that I wanted to create a large company with multiple divisions, all based around my core values, with the things that had helped me to heal at the very heart of it.

Spurred on by hard-earned self-belief, my husband Paul's unwavering support, and a determination to create something truly special and give back to the community that had been part of my journey, in October 2011, shortly before I turned 31, mymuybueno was born.

> I wanted a business that would enable me to have the family I had always dreamed of, and to give my children the childhood I had been denied. And I knew I was capable of doing it.

My life up until this point had, I realised, all been leading to this. As I travelled the world, working on super yachts and learning from others, I gained confidence as well as expertise, and it was from all this exposure to so many different walks of life that my vision began to emerge.

I wanted to combine everything: the things I had learnt, the person I had become, my dreams, beliefs, passions and values, to create a business that encompassed it all. I wanted a business that would enable me to have the family I had always dreamed of, and to give my children the childhood I had been denied. And I knew I was capable of doing it.

Each division of mymuybueno launched one at a time so that I could create solid foundations for that vision; it was about doing things properly or not at all. I started the deli out of my own kitchen and won gold Great Taste Awards for my strawberry conserve and granola (see the recipes in my Breakfast chapter) each time I entered them. We were soon a multi-award-winning deli thanks to a commitment that meant always using the best ingredients and cooking them with love.

The mymuybueno Private Chefs agency came about from my experience as a chef working on super yachts, where there was a distinct lack of representation. I knew the role inside out, which enabled me to represent other chefs and find them their next job while in turn knowing precisely what my clients were seeking. I always looked at it like match-making, hand-selecting individuals based on their merits and handling their careers long-term. We are now one of the biggest private chef agencies in the world.

With a primary focus on connecting people and making world-class chefs accessible, I then created an online brand presence through Instagram, launching a platform called mymuybueno Chefs. The idea is for chefs from all over the globe to share their dishes, inspiring and exciting one another, alongside interviews in mymuybueno Chefs Get Personal, which enables chefs and foodies around the world to connect. Bringing these very chefs to the mymuybueno Cookery School in Palma really brings the circle together, teaching students and establishing a special community of good people who love good food. Building the community with the use of our own #mymuybuenochefs hashtag is really uniting individuals with the same passion.

My vision for mymuybueno continued to grow, gradually creating new divisions for interior crew placement such as butlers and stewardesses, luxury flatware, elite concierge services and bespoke luxury catering. Never compromising on the 'my' in mymuybueno, which represents my core values and ensures they are evident in everything we do, meant that my business quickly gained a reputation for quality, reliability, truly personalised service and, always, good food. Today we have seven different divisions within the mymuybueno Group.

It was food once again that really set me free.

By writing this book and sharing the mymuybueno world with you, I hope that I can make a difference in your life with good food too. My relationship with food has always been such a pronounced one, and as that relationship changed, from being a weapon to becoming a lifeline; from being a source of pain and ill health to one of joy and vitality, I repeatedly found that good food and good people were pulling me back from my darkest times. Eventually, it was food once again that really set me free. Cooking at home and for friends, hosting dinner parties, making roast dinners and just seeing the enjoyment they could offer never failed to make me happy.

However, to tell you how I got to that happy place, I have to go back to the very beginning, when my life looked very much the opposite of what it does today. I didn't have friends, or a warm and loving family; my childhood was a cold and isolated one. My parents were not the kind and loving sort, but violent towards each other, and towards me. This resulted in me living through an extremely unhappy childhood, full of physical and emotional abuse.

Food played a very negative part in my life
during those early years.

Food played a very negative part in my life during those early years. We never ate as a family; it was always a lonely and isolating experience, and one that my mother wielded as a weapon. I was often forced to eat, and mealtimes usually resulted in some form of punishment for a perceived misdemeanour, yet I was also never fed properly, existing instead on a diet of deep-fried foods and little else. This, unsurprisingly, led to me developing an eating disorder, and as I got a little older I found ways to hide and dispose of my meals, meaning I was seriously underfed and malnourished.

I was nine years-old when my father left, and in contrast to the relief that might have brought, my mother's behaviour became considerably more disturbing. The years that followed were deeply unhappy, and my overwhelming memory of this time in my life is knowing that I needed to escape, and of being forced, as a child, to plan for ways in which I might do so. An instinct for survival kicked in.

I will forever be grateful to her, not only for showing me
love, but also for showing me the power and importance
of good food, and the positive impact that it can have on
one's life

There was some light in this dark period. At the age of 13, I got my first job working weekends and holidays at a shellfish bar in Cornwall, where I was living at the time. The lady who ran it, a kind and loving woman, recognised the life I was living and took me under her wing. She fabricated reasons that would enable me to spend occasional evenings at her house, being embraced into the fold of her family. She loved to cook, and it was here that I learned about real food, and real ingredients. She would cook all sorts of wonderful things; things I'd never seen, experienced or eaten before in my life, and I would stand in her kitchen, fascinated and enthralled, desperate to learn as much as possible. It was here that I first felt a sense of belonging and what family truly meant. I will forever be grateful to her, not only for showing me love, but also for showing me the power and importance of good food, and the positive impact that it can have on one's life, especially when enjoyed alongside those you love.

I was 14 when I finally escaped from my mother's house, realising – following an incident with her latest boyfriend – that it was a necessary act of survival. It is a day that is forever etched on my memory as one of horror and trauma, and was also the last time I ever saw my mother. This crossroad in my life took me back to my father, with whom I lived for a short while before his true colours were shown again, and I found myself being thrown into a life of self-sufficiency at the age of 16.

The restaurant invested in training me and once again I found myself learning as much as I could.

This, however, was the point at which food came back into my life as a form of salvation, when I found a wonderful job at a restaurant. I loved the people I was working with, I was fed every day, and for the first time in a long time, I felt happy. The restaurant invested in training me and once again I found myself learning as much as I could about food, and discovering the positive influence that it had on my life. It was during this period that things finally started to go in the right direction for me. I started to find myself surrounded by kind people, including my granny, who I was finally able to get to know after escaping from my mother, and who, over the following years, became an incredibly important part of my life, and truly my best friend. It was also during this time that I was given the opportunity to move into another family's home, where I was welcomed and cared for, before eventually moving into a flatshare with friends from work, ready to put my past fully behind me at the age of 18.

I had a sense of belonging and safety in the presence of chefs, kitchens and food.

Unfortunately, the years of abuse and neglect had left me vulnerable and with a lot of life skills to learn. I found myself going into free fall, experiencing mounting debts, trusting people I shouldn't, and ultimately being subjected to further abuse. It is the period of my life I still find hardest to talk about, and one during which I was pulled into a darkness that I still struggle to comprehend. However, I found the strength to escape, and once again it was in a restaurant, surrounded by good food, and good people, that I found my salvation. I had a sense of belonging and safety in the presence of chefs, kitchens and food, and it was this period of time, I have no doubt, which cemented my future and facilitated the self-sufficiency that enabled me to become the woman I am today.

I enjoyed a number of happy years working at the restaurant, until a horrific experience at the hands of a colleague changed that overnight. It no longer felt like a safe place, so I left the company and embarked again on the pursuit of happiness and a better life. At the age of 25, I was ready to make a completely new start. My faith was strong and I was no longer afraid of the world. In fact, I wanted to go out there and meet it, explore it, and taste it. Having previously met someone who worked on a super yacht as a private chef, travelling the world and cooking for a living, I knew exactly what I wanted to do. Spending every last penny I had, I completed the necessary courses and certifications, and then in September 2006 booked a one-way ticket to Palma de Mallorca in order to chase my dream.

My faith was strong and I was no longer afraid of the world.
In fact, I wanted to go out there and meet it, explore it,
and taste it.

By the end of my first day walking the docks to find work, I had the opportunity to interview, by cooking a three-course meal, for a job on a private motor yacht. Putting every ounce of passion, heart and soul into the meal, I succeeded in landing the job. The position was incredible, and although it was hard work, I experienced a freedom unlike anything I could have imagined. This job was the first of many in the industry, and the years that followed allowed me to explore the Mediterranean and the Caribbean, discovering the joys of local markets and fresh colourful produce while enhancing my skills and cementing my passion for cooking.

I eventually moved onto sailing yachts, and it was here that I really fell in love. The memories I have of spending time up on deck, watching dolphins chase the boat, and seeing sunrises and sunsets I could only have dreamed about before, will stay close to my heart forever. I was so humbled by how my life couldn't be further from anything I had ever experienced before, cooking for some of the world's most wealthy individuals and visiting amazing places.

One of the hardest parts of working and living on yachts was being so far from my granny, because she was getting older and I was scared that I wouldn't be around if something happened. When she passed, I was so very upset, but grateful that I had been able to return quickly enough to say goodbye. She always told me that one day I would meet a man just like my grandpa, someone who would love me for me, and treat me with respect and love. Within a few weeks of her passing, the next yacht I secured a job on was the very place I met the man my granny had described. It was as if she went to heaven and conspired with God to make that happen for me.

I finally had stability, for the very first time in my life.

Paul was unlike any man I had been with before, and by the end of our first official date I knew he was the person I would spend the rest of my life with. We lived and worked together over the next two years, blissfully happy, and in 2010, Paul and I married. I finally had stability, for the very first time in my life. Being with Paul, secure in the knowledge that he truly loved me, and working in my dream job as a chef, had given me tremendous strength, and I finally felt able to cut all ties with everyone who had ever hurt me. Trusting in people was, and still is, very hard for me, but together we knew we were able to face anything. Surrounding ourselves with good people, we set about building a life that was free of any hurt, stress or drama.

It took time, but after overcoming some further hurdles including an eating disorder, I started to live my life in a much happier way, no longer struggling with my demons, refusing to compromise on my happiness or tolerate any bad people around me. Paul and I were working together on a yacht for a wonderful family who inspired me greatly, and it was at this point that I started to have a vision for being self-employed and running my own business, which would become mymuybueno.

Mallorca had long since become our home by this point; the yachts had repeatedly bought us back here and we'd fallen further in love with the island every time. This beautiful place was not only where we knew we wanted to put down roots and start a family, it was also the inspiration for my business. Seeing gaps in the market I wanted to fill, it was the place that had allowed me to change my life so completely, and so there was never any doubt that this Spanish island was where I wanted to establish mymuybueno. It was important for that to be somehow reflected in the business' name, and so 'muy bueno' – the Spanish for 'very good' and a phrase associated with eating food – was combined with the equally important 'my' to create mymuybueno, a brand to evoke good food, the personal touch, and both a British and Spanish heritage with an immense amount of heart in its meaning.

It was in the third year of the business, during the height of mymuybueno's initial growth spurt, that Paul and I welcomed our first son into the world. Life threw yet another hurdle my way in the form of birth complications, due to excessive force used by the doctor, that led to the nerves in Seth's arm being snapped, resulting in him being born with a condition called Erb's Palsy. Consequently, since his very first weeks, he has required daily physiotherapy and has had to endure multiple surgeries, the first of which he had at just four months old and which will continue throughout his life. Becoming a mother and starting a family meant everything to me, and despite the challenges of juggling a growing business with being a new mother, often alone, with Paul away for work, in addition to everything that came with Seth's condition, by having only good people in my life I was able to survive this difficult time, and ultimately it gave me a drive to succeed that was stronger than ever.

Since becoming a mother, I have focused even more on the importance of what we put into our bodies.

Eighteen months after Seth was born, we welcomed Jacob into the world, completing our family. It was important for me to give Seth a sibling, and because his birth had been such a traumatic experience, I knew that if I didn't do it soon, I may not have wanted to at all. This time, I was able to enjoy all the moments that had been missed before, and as the business grew, we also decided it was the perfect opportunity for Paul to join mymuybueno and take on the financial and compliance side of the company. This meant that he would be home permanently, alleviating some of my workload. Having his support, and his belief in my vision from the very beginning, has been everything: he's been my rock and is my best friend.

Since becoming a mother, I have focused even more on the importance of what we put into our bodies. The impact I saw processed sugar have on my children horrified me, and having such a responsibility for what I put in their bodies, and also my own, I sought alternatives.

I believe in 'everything in moderation' and being able to enjoy a dessert in a restaurant or sweets now and then, but on a daily basis for everyday eating, not using refined sugar is hugely important to me as part of having a healthy relationship with food.

It was crucial that all my bakes tasted just as delicious as they did with eggs, butter, sugar and cream, and over many years of tweaking and testing (and our dogs having tray after tray of discarded attempts) I have created so many amazing cakes, sweet bites and raw desserts which are super decadent, yet totally guilt-free. I believe in 'everything in moderation' and being able to enjoy a dessert in a restaurant or sweets now and then, but on a daily basis for everyday eating, not using refined sugar is hugely important to me as part of having a healthy relationship with food.

Eventually, I redefined the entire mymuybueno Deli so as to make it accessible to everyone with a menu that is completely plant-based, gluten-free, dairy-free and refined sugar-free, all created from the perspective of a chef, food lover and mother.

Through hard work, commitment and a refusal to compromise on my core values, I had created a successful and ever-expanding international business. However, it was at this point that I knew I needed to focus on really utilising what I had built in order to make a difference, and to give back to the community that had been, in so many ways, my salvation. Beginning to share my story, and seeing the power and effect that had, inspired me to start the mymuybueno Women in Business Day in 2017. This yearly event is about sharing my personal story, how I built mymuybueno, business advice and my methods, all with the aim of motivating others.

The focus is to inspire and empower women, to equip them to do the same thing I had done: build the life they deserve. Following this, I also created a monthly breakfast event bringing like-minded women in business together, to provide a platform for sharing, empowering, strengthening, inspiring and supporting each other. Community is at the heart of everything I do, connected by good food and good people.

My life and journey have been full of challenges, but all these experiences have moulded me, and through mymuybueno I have created a safe place to work and live. I escaped from extreme adversity multiple times, determined to build the life and family I always dreamed of, and I work hard every single day to nurture and grow them both, living by what I now call the mymuybueno philosophy. I've created a company which is effectively all about helping people: feeding them, teaching them, bringing them together, finding them jobs, all with a connecting thread of food. Life is busy, and juggling being a mother to both my boys with home life, my business and my ever-growing teams is a lot of hard work, but no matter how full my days are, breaking bread with the people I love is at the heart of everything, and it is that which gives me so much joy.

This is a book to inspire you to keep believing,
and to remind you that it's never too late
to start living the life that you deserve.

I really want to help others achieve the same. I want to remind people that no matter what you have been through, you can be anything you want to be with hard work, a passion for what you do, and a refusal to compromise on the things that you believe in. With this book, I hope that I am able to do so. I want it to be a practical guide: a book you can pick up and read, and cook from, every day. The only cookbook you will ever need, and a book that will not only enable you to enjoy good and healthy food with your loved ones, but also build your confidence in the kitchen, remind you that you too have the ability to achieve your dreams, and help you to live your best life, no matter how many times it takes to get there, and no matter what you have gone through before. This is a book to inspire you to keep believing, and to remind you that it's never too late to start living the life that you deserve. I hope you enjoy The mymuybueno Cookbook as much as I enjoyed creating it.

mymuybueno®

Core Values

Pride, Integrity, Ambition, Passion and Love.

Philosophy

Always cross your t's and dot your i's.

Never ever run before you can walk.

Get your ducks in a row,
being organised keeps you in control.

Do it properly, or don't do it at all,
from the small to the big things.

Work hard, you get out what you put in.

Never compromise on your core values,
they should dictate everything you do and
every decision that you make.

Remove all the naysayers, only surround
yourself with people who lift you up.

If you want to do something, you'll do it.
If not, you'll make excuses. Stop making excuses.

About this book

It was important for me to make a cookbook that was really practical, equipping my readers to easily make all the dishes within it and enjoy the confidence that cooking them will bring. All of my recipes are timesaving as well as delicious, and I've tested, retested and tweaked each of them many times to ensure they will work for you perfectly, every time. These are recipes you can make again and again, always with ease and enjoyment.

Whether this is a cookbook you keep in your kitchen, take with you to the sofa or even to bed at night to plan your meals for the day or week ahead, I want it to be one that you can turn to time and again for ideas and inspiration.

The vast majority of my recipes are very easy to adapt, making this a book for everyone. You can simply exchange meat or fish for vegetables, or remove cheese, so that if you are vegetarian or vegan you can easily make a minor change that will enable you to enjoy the dish too. All recipes have been tested with gluten-free flour too, so this is another easy swap to make.

It's also full of my tips to help you to get your ducks in a row, be organised and in control, because life is so busy. We cram so much into our day. This will enable you to better manage your time, making it more realistic to cook every day, and spend quality time with those you love, eating and enjoying good food together.

So many of our bad habits have evolved from poor diets and a lack of self-love, so I have created this book in the hopes of helping you to really fall in love with food, and the joy of sharing it with the good people around you.

For me the balance is about eating healthily, but also not depriving yourself. Have healthy juices and nourishing breakfast bowls, but also to allow yourself to enjoy bacon and eggs, or pizza or cheese or chocolate when you want to, as long as it's in moderation. Enjoying a balance between all the meals you eat is key, and by following the recipes in this book you can do so with ease, because, as you are making it all from scratch, you know exactly what goes into each and every meal.

After many years of abusing my body, and then after having two children, my body is not the same as it once was. I have to take more care about what goes into it, but it's also important not to beat myself up when I do have some sort of indulgence. I love food and I love eating out, and I don't deprive myself of enjoying a nice dessert in a restaurant, but I'll make sure I get the balance back the next day by juicing or having lighter, healthier meals.

I have a very sweet tooth; I love having something to satisfy those sugary cravings, but I also have a responsibility to my children and what I put inside their bodies, as well as what I put inside mine. Not using refined sugar in any of my recipes means you can feel less guilty about your sweet treats, and are more in control of what you are putting into your body, and those around you.

I have perfected my desserts so that they taste like they are full of butter, eggs, cream and sugar, while in fact being 100% plant-based. I wanted everything to taste just as my original deli produce does, from a chef's perspective, but also as a mummy. My boys have taste-tested every one of my desserts and bakes over the years, so when I 'fooled' them and got the thumbs up, which took a great many attempts, their honest feedback helped me to settle on my final recipes. I made tray after tray of cakes for months in order to tweak and refine, so as to achieve exactly the right texture and flavours. And when it tastes so good, why would you ever need to go back to eating sweet desserts any other way at home?

Our palates also adjust; I see it in my boys too. When we do have some sweets, shop-bought ice cream or a dessert out, it's often just too sweet and my teeth hurt, so we have them much less often, and definitely don't crave or miss them.

Being able to just enjoy eating better, and to care more about what goes in your body without needing to label things makes a big difference. You don't need to be vegan to enjoy plant-based desserts. I'm not vegan and have no food intolerances: I just want to eat well and be healthy, but I love food.

I want this book to be a tool for good living. My goal is to encourage finding the time to really stop, sit down and break bread, by making dishes that enable us to have a healthy relationship with both food and people, and to take the time in our busy lives to enjoy those precious moments, and in turn live happier and healthier lives.

Pantry & Equipment

Being well stocked up is essential. Below is a complete list of all the ingredients and equipment used in this book. The dry goods, spices, natural sweeteners, nuts, seeds and oils will take time to build up but once you have everything to hand, you will be able to make most dishes in this book conveniently.

For gluten-free diets, buy specifically gluten-free flour, baking agents, oats, brown rice pasta, and tamari. All my recipes have been tested to work with these ingredients too.

I use a fan-assisted oven for all baking, and change it to a roasting setting for vegetables and meat or fish.

Dried Herbs and Spices

Black peppercorns
Cardamom pods
Cayenne pepper
Chilli flakes
Chilli powder
Cinnamon sticks
Cloves
Cumin seeds
Curry powder
Dried finger chillies
Dried oregano
Dried parsley
Dried thyme
Fennel seeds
Garam masala
Garlic powder
Ground cinnamon
Ground coriander
Ground cumin
Ground ginger
Ground nutmeg
Ground turmeric
Ground white pepper
Mixed spice
Mustard seeds
Nigella seeds
Onion powder
Paprika
Saffron strands
Smoked paprika
Star anise
Whole nutmeg

Sauces and Pastes

Brown rice miso
Dijon mustard
Fish sauce
Horseradish
Shrimp paste
Soy sauce
Tahini
Tamarind paste
Tomato purée
Wasabi
White miso

Dry Goods

Arrowroot
Baking powder
Bicarbonate of soda
Dried yeast
Jumbo rolled oats
Plain flour
Self-raising flour
Semolina flour
Tipo 00 flour
Xanthan gum

Cupboard

Anchovy fillets
Apple cider vinegar
Balsamic vinegar
Brown rice
Capers
Couscous
Dried flat rice noodles
Dried green or brown lentils
Espresso coffee
Flaked sea salt
Flour or corn tortillas
Good quality tinned full fat coconut milk
Himalayan salt
Jasmine or basmati rice
Kalamata olives
Malt vinegar
Nori sheets
Nutritional yeast
Paella rice
Panko breadcrumbs
Passata (sugar-free)
Pickled ginger
Pomegranate molasses
Quinoa
Ramen noodles
Red wine
Red wine vinegar
Rice paper wrappers
Rice vinegar
Spaghetti, or any shape of pasta
Sun-dried tomatoes
Sushi rice
Tinned black beans
Tinned brown lentils
Tinned cannellini beans
Tinned chickpeas
Tinned chopped tomatoes
Togarashi
Vegetable, chicken, beef and lamb stock
White wine
White wine vinegar

Oils

Coconut oil (deodorised)
Olive oil
Sesame oil
Sunflower oil

Seeds

Buckwheat
Chia seeds
Ground flaxseed/linseed
Psyllium husk
Pumpkin seeds
Sesame seeds
Sunflower seeds
Whole flaxseed/linseed

Nuts

Cashews
Flaked almonds
Ground almonds
Macadamias
Peanuts
Pecans
Pistachios
Whole almonds

Fruit and Vegetables

Asparagus
Aubergine
Avocados
Baby spinach
Bananas
Beetroot
Blueberries
Broccoli and tenderstem broccoli
Butternut squash
Carrots
Cauliflower
Celery
Cherry tomatoes
Chestnut mushrooms
Corn on the cob
Courgette
Cucumber
Figs
Fresh herbs: dill, parsley, basil, coriander, mint, chives, bay leaves, rosemary, thyme, Thai basil
Galangal
Garlic

Gem lettuce
Ginger
Golden Delicious apples
Green beans
Kale
Kohlrabi
Leeks
Lemons
Limes
Mangetout
Mango
Mixed leaves
Oranges
Pak choi
Pineapples
Pomegranate
Radishes
Raspberries
Red and brown onions
Red and green bird's eye chillies
Red and white cabbage
Red and yellow bell peppers
Rocket
Shallots
Shiitake mushrooms
Spring onions
Strawberries
Sweet potatoes
Vine tomatoes
White potatoes

Freezer

Baby dried shrimps
Filo pastry
Ginger or galangal
Gyoza wrappers
Ice cubes
Kaffir lime leaves
Lemongrass
Mixed berries (strawberries, blueberries, raspberries)
Peas
Ripe avocados, peeled and quartered
Ripe bananas, peeled and sliced

Fridge

Buffalo mozzarella
Butter
Carton milks (sugar-free almond, rice, coconut)
Coconut yoghurt
Cream cheese
Eggs (free-range)
Feta
Greek yoghurt (natural, sugar-free)

Mayonnaise
Parmesan cheese block
Single cream

Natural Sweeteners and Flavourings

Almond butter
Blackstrap molasses
Brown rice syrup
Cacao paste (in rounds)
Cacao butter (in rounds)
Cacao nibs
Coconut butter
Coconut flakes
Coconut milk
Coconut sugar
Desiccated coconut
Dried cranberries
Dried sultanas
Hazelnut butter
Local runny honey
Medjool dates, pitted (one pitted date is approximately 20g)
Orange extract
Palm sugar
Peanut butter
Peppermint extract
Pure maple syrup
Vanilla paste or extract

Powders

Acai powder
Blueberry powder
Maca powder
Matcha green tea powder (ceremonial)
Raspberry powder
Raw cacao powder
Reishi powder
Spirulina powder
Vanilla powder (¼ of a teaspoon is the equivalent of one teaspoon of paste or extract)
Wheatgrass powder

Meat, Fish and Seafood

Beef fillet
Chicken breasts, thighs and wings
Chorizo
Clams
Lamb shoulder and leg
Langoustines
Mussels
Oxtail
Prawns
Salmon
Sea bass
Serrano ham

Smoked salmon
Squid
Whole chicken

Equipment

20cm round cake tin (loose-bottomed)
20cm sandwich cake tins
20cm tart tin (loose-bottomed)
2lb loaf tin
Angled palette knife
Aluminium foil
Baking trays
Balloon whisk
Box grater
Chopping boards
Chopsticks
Cling film
Colander
Cooling rack
Digital timer
Doughnut baking tin
Dutch oven or casserole dish with lid
Electric Milk frother
Fish tweezers
Griddle pan
Ice cream scoop (½ cup size)
Ice lolly moulds
Immersion blender
Kitchen paper
Kitchen string
Knives (bread, cook's, tomato, paring)
Ladle
Large palette knife
Large saucepan with lid
Matcha bamboo whisk
Measuring spoons
Meat thermometer
Melon baller
Metal sieve (for wet use)
Microplane grater
Mini silicone ice cream moulds
Mixing bowls (large, medium and small)
Muffin tin
Non-stick frying pan
Nut milk bag
Oven trays
Paella pan
Parchment paper
Pepper grinder
Pestle and mortar
Piping bags and nozzle
Plastic sieve (for dry use)
Potato masher

Potato peeler
Pyrex medium bowl
Roasting tin
Rolling pin
Scissors
Sealable bags
Silicone doughnut moulds
Silicone pastry brush
Silicone spatula
Skewers (metal and bamboo)
Slotted spoon
Small palette knife (this is useful for everything)
Small ramekins
Small saucepan with lid
Spice grinder
Square or rectangular brownie tin
Stock pot with lid
Sushi rolling mat
Tea towels
Tongs
Toothpicks
Weighing scales
Wire cooling rack
Wooden ice lolly sticks
Wooden spoons
Zester

Blender

A Vitamix is ideal for the cheesecakes, but other blenders will work and just need to run for longer

Electric Stand Mixer

KitchenAid (with the paddle, whisk and dough hook attachments)

Food Processor

A Magimix is the best investment you'll ever make

Ice Cream Machine

Not essential; you can just freeze the nice cream in a tub and thaw it for a little longer

Start your day the mymuybueno way

These first two chapters cover a hugely important part of your day, as getting breakfast right really impacts the rest of it. If I am organised and give myself the time to sit and enjoy breakfast, I tend to start my morning on the right foot. I usually find that things work out better. I'm in control, I feel good, I have clarity, I feel sustained and eat well throughout the day.

For many of us, time is a real issue. As a busy mum, just trying to get out of the door in the morning is a constant challenge, and sometimes the reality is just grabbing a banana to eat on the go. But the more organised I am, the better things run and the more I can accomplish, meaning I can make a difference to both my day and my family's.

Making certain things in advance such as a tub of almond butter, a big jar of granola or my ultra seedy bread helps you to be one step ahead. Being organised is a huge part of helping you to make better food choices and eating better while enjoying a balance.

My house is always full of bananas, and once they start to really ripen, I peel and freeze them. You can slice them up first, as they then break down easier in your processor or blender. If you want to use them right away, it's a perfect time to make muffins or banana bread as a treat.

Being organised is a huge part of helping you to make better food choices and eating better while enjoying a balance.

I also keep my freezer full of frozen berries and even avocados (for the green juice) as well as pitted Medjool dates. Then it's all right there, ready to use when you want to make something, and also means you have less waste. When things are starting to ripen and you haven't had time to use them, just peel it, pit it and freeze it.

The acai recipe in this chapter is my favourite bowl of goodness; it gives you so much energy and a real spring in your step. It's also super quick to put together when you have all the ingredients ready.

My fridge has always got a big pot of chia pudding and overnight oats inside, for when I am short on time. It's easy to pop some into a bowl to feed my boys and nourish myself, before jumping feet first into my day. When I have more time, or it's a weekend, we get to enjoy some pancakes together, which always go down well.

Sometimes I just want some comfort and really fancy scrambled eggs with smoked salmon or crispy bacon; other times I love having a soft-boiled egg with avocado on toast. You can really mix and match how you please and find a balance that works for you.

In the Dips, Dressings & Staples chapter you'll find my almond and coconut milk recipes, which are so delicious that once you try them, you'll want to make them more often.

> You can mix and match how you please and find a balance that works for you.

I also use almond milk from a carton at home, and in my deli, we use rice and coconut milk too. You can use oat milk if you're not gluten-free. Just ensure you read the labels to make sure there is no sugar added.

I have veered away from using cow's milk over the years, and you'll notice that I don't use it in this book at all. I found that when I stopped using cow's milk, my psoriasis also stopped, which I had struggled with for many years. I like dairy but in moderation.

I enjoy Greek yoghurt and I love eggs, although they must be good quality, and always free-range. I use both in my muffins and pancakes, but I have also shared my plant-based alternatives.

I like to start my day on an empty stomach with a cold-pressed juice, using a masticating juicer. If you don't already have one, this would be one of the best investments you can make, as you will use it every day. I find that starting my day with a juice dictates the rest of my day's eating habits. It hydrates me and makes me feel good, and if I am dedicated to juicing daily, it keeps away any flu-type symptoms. If ever I have a period where I don't juice, I often come down with something, meaning I then need to up the dosage of lemon and ginger. Juicing is the best way to easily give my children all the vegetables and nutrients they need, and (better still) because each juice tastes so good, they don't even realise.

Drinking juices to cleanse my body really works if I've had a lot of food, like at Christmas time, or if I've been eating out or simply overindulging. It's also good for when I feel full and clogged and just want to reset my body and give my digestive tract a rest. I always feel so much lighter for it. Once juicing becomes part of your morning ritual, you will really feel the difference.

> Once juicing becomes part of your morning ritual, you will really feel the difference.

The hot drinks are all my favourite blends that also make you feel good. As a ridiculously busy woman who consumes a huge amount of coffee, having these blends helps me to unwind and take a break from coffee. I always find them comforting at any time of day.

Whether sweet or savoury, these chapters are full of ideas to help you to start your day the mymuybueno way: realistically, and with ease.

Breakfast

granola

This granola was my first ever mymuybueno Deli recipe back in 2011, and has won every time I've entered the Great Taste Awards since that first year. It's simply delicious with sliced banana, fresh berries, a dollop of nutobutter and milk, or as a topping for your acai, chia pudding or yoghurt bowl. This recipe makes a nice big batch to last for a while.

2 tbsp sunflower oil
150g maple syrup
1 tbsp honey or brown rice syrup
1 tsp vanilla extract or paste
320g jumbo rolled oats
50g sunflower seeds
55g sesame seeds
60g pumpkin seeds
80g flaked almonds
50g dried sultanas
50g dried cranberries
40g coconut flakes

Preheat your oven to 150°c while you mix the oil, maple syrup, honey or brown rice syrup and vanilla in a large bowl. Tip in all the remaining ingredients except the dried fruit and coconut, and mix well.

Pour the granola onto two baking sheets and spread it out evenly. Bake for 15 minutes in the preheated oven, then remove and push the granola around the tray so that any uncooked oat mixture will be exposed to the heat.

Stir in the sultanas, cranberries and coconut flakes well then bake for 10 to 15 minutes until golden brown. Be very careful not to let the fruit burn.

Remove the trays from the oven and push the granola mixture around again, so that it doesn't stick together or to the tray while cooling. Do this every so often until the granola has cooled completely.

The granola can be stored in an airtight container for up to a month.

acai

I love this combination so much. It's mymuybueno Deli's biggest selling breakfast bowl in the summer months, so colourful and it really gives you a mega boost to energise your day, at any time. My boys adore it, as it's like having ice cream for breakfast. You can top it with granola, nut butter, yoghurt, mixed seeds, fresh fruit – whatever you wish – or just enjoy it as it comes.

1 frozen banana, sliced
150g mixed frozen berries (such as blueberries, strawberries and raspberries)
1 tsp acai powder
¼ tsp maca powder
½ tbsp cacao powder
60ml almond milk
1 tbsp almond butter
2 Medjool dates, pitted

Place all the ingredients in a high speed blender and pulse until you've reached a soft serve consistency. You want a semi-frozen finish, so resist adding more liquid and instead just keep blending to force the frozen fruit to break down.

Serve immediately. Be sure to eat it straight away before it melts. Enjoy.

vanilla chia pudding

SERVES 2

This is in my fridge permanently. It's so quick and easy to make last thing in the evening before putting the house to bed, meaning you have a guaranteed breakfast in the fridge at all times, which is a lifesaver on busy days. I love a bowl of this at any time of day as it's a really satisfying pick me up, and because it gives you amazing energy.

4 tbsp chia seeds
250ml almond milk
120g coconut yoghurt or Greek yoghurt
¼ tsp vanilla powder
2 tsp brown rice syrup, maple syrup or honey

To make the vanilla chia pudding, place the chia seeds in a bowl with the milk and yoghurt. Whisk the mixture with a fork to break up the chia seeds, which will all clump together.

Add the vanilla and your syrup of choice, or honey, then whisk well again.

Leave the pudding to set in the fridge overnight.

Enjoy the next day with the toppings of your choice.

overnight oats

SERVES 1

Much like the chia pudding, making this the night before means you always have a great breakfast in the fridge. It's filling and comforting too, especially warmed through in a saucepan over the winter months. These are my favourite flavours, but you can also try apple and cinnamon or fresh raspberries with cacao powder, which are all delicious ingredients to play with; swap until you discover the combination you love most.

Banana and Cinnamon
1 ripe banana
1 tbsp chia seeds
¼ tsp ground cinnamon
50g jumbo rolled oats
185ml almond milk
¼ tsp vanilla powder
Pinch of Himalayan salt

Nut Butter and Sultana
50g jumbo rolled oats
1 tbsp chia seeds
2 tbsp almond or peanut butter
1 tbsp maple syrup
2 tbsp sultanas
185ml almond milk
Pinch of Himalayan salt

Banana and Cinnamon

In a bowl, mash the banana until almost smooth. Now stir in the chia seeds and cinnamon until combined. Stir in the oats, almond milk, vanilla and salt. Cover and refrigerate overnight.

In the morning, stir the oat mixture to combine everything. If it's runny, simply stir in one additional tablespoon of chia seeds and place the mixture back in the fridge until it has thickened up. If the oat mixture is too thick, simply add a splash of milk and stir to combine.

Nut Butter and Sultana

In a bowl, mix the oats, chia seeds, nut butter, maple syrup, sultanas, milk and salt together. Cover and refrigerate overnight.

In the morning, stir the oat mixture to combine everything. If it's runny, simply stir in one additional tablespoon of chia seeds and place the mixture back in the fridge until it has thickened up. If the oat mixture is too thick, simply add a splash of milk and stir to combine.

maple, pecan and banana muffins

MAKES 12

Maple, pecan and banana are a combination that really works. These muffins are extremely moist and taste amazing. Ensure your bananas are really ripe as otherwise the muffins will be drier and less sweet.

150g coconut sugar
75g coconut oil, melted
2 tbsp maple syrup
400g ripe bananas (approx. 4 medium size)
220g self-raising flour
3 tsp baking powder
1 tsp ground cinnamon
Pinch of Himalayan salt
80g pecan nuts, ground to a flour

For the topping
1 tbsp chopped pecan nuts
1 tbsp coconut sugar

Preheat your oven to 180°c and line your muffin tin with cases.

Use a electric stand mixer with a paddle attachment to make the batter. Put the coconut sugar, melted coconut oil and maple syrup into the bowl and leave to mix for around 5 minutes so everything is well incorporated and all the sugar has melted. You can of course do this by hand instead, with a wooden spoon.

In a separate bowl, mash the ripe bananas and add it into the mixture, allowing it to blend in well for a few minutes.

Put the self-raising flour, baking powder, cinnamon, salt and ground pecans into a separate bowl and mix well, then gently fold the flour mixture into the wet mixture by hand with a spatula. Don't overmix the batter otherwise your muffins will be hard.

Use an ice cream scoop to place even amounts of batter into each muffin case, and then top each one with some chopped pecans and a touch of coconut sugar.

Bake the muffins for 20 minutes in the preheated oven, then leave them to cool in the tin for 10 minutes before moving each one to a wire rack to cool completely.

blueberry muffins

MAKES 12

Light, fluffy, and seriously addictive. It's quite hard to stop at just one with these because they are just so good. I find myself having to freeze half the batch so they aren't demolished in one day.

350g plain flour
3 tsp baking powder
Pinch of Himalayan salt
200g coconut sugar
2 eggs
240ml Greek yoghurt
120ml sunflower oil
1 tsp vanilla extract or paste
225g blueberries, fresh or frozen

Preheat your oven to 220°c and line your muffin tin with cases.

Weigh the flour, baking powder, salt and coconut sugar into a bowl, then stir to combine. Whisk the eggs, yoghurt, oil and vanilla together in a second bowl.

Pour the wet ingredients into the dry and mix gently until combined. Don't overmix the batter otherwise your muffins will be hard. Put all of your blueberries into the batter and carefully stir them through.

Use an ice cream scoop to place even amounts of batter into each muffin case. Make sure they are filled three quarters of the way up and you evenly distribute the mix so there are blueberries in each case.

Bake the muffins on the middle shelf for 25 minutes until golden brown. Leave to cool for 10 minutes in the tin, and then move your muffins to a wire rack to cool completely. Enjoy.

banana bread

SERVES 8

Nothing is better than filling the house with the smell of freshly baked banana bread. This is a firm favourite at mymuybueno Deli and always sells out when it's on display. It's gorgeous on its own, or slathered with peanut butter and strawberry conserve for a really wonderful treat.

For the flax egg
1 tbsp ground flaxseed
3 tbsp warm water

Wet Ingredients
55ml coconut oil, plus extra for greasing
400g ripe bananas (approx. 4 medium size)
80ml almond milk
2 tbsp maple syrup
1 tsp vanilla extract or paste

Dry ingredients
65g coconut sugar
60g jumbo rolled oats
1 tsp bicarbonate of soda
½ tsp baking powder
½ tsp Himalayan salt
280g self-raising flour
1 whole banana, sliced (no end bits)

Preheat the oven to 180°c and grease your 2lb loaf tin lightly with coconut oil using a silicone brush.

First make your 'flax egg'. Mix the flaxseed with the warm water and leave for 10 minutes to thicken.

Meanwhile, melt your coconut oil in a saucepan. In a large bowl, mash the banana until almost smooth, then stir the flax egg, milk, melted coconut oil, maple syrup and vanilla into the mashed banana until well combined.

Stir the dry ingredients into the batter one at a time, mixing well to incorporate each before adding the next. Add the coconut sugar first to ensure it melts, then the oats, bicarbonate of soda, baking powder, salt and lastly the flour.

Ensure everything is mixed well and there are no patches of flour. This is very important, as otherwise you will get white splodges in the bread and they do not taste good.

Pour the batter into the prepared loaf tin and spread out evenly. Place the sliced banana across the top in the row along the centre and gently push down.

Bake the loaf, uncovered, for 45 minutes, until lightly golden and firm on top. If it starts to caramelise and darken the bananas on top too much (if your bananas were really ripe and therefore had more sugar content, this will happen) simply cover with a sheet of dampened scrunched up parchment paper to protect the top from burning.

After 45 minutes, check that the loaf is cooked through using a skewer. If it is ready, this should come out clean, and the top of the loaf should slowly spring back when touched.

Leave the loaf in the tin for 10 minutes to cool. Do not leave it any longer as it will sweat and make your loaf damp and prone to breakage. Slide a palette knife around the edges to loosen them, and gently remove it from the tin. Place your banana bread onto a wire rack and leave until completely cooled.

ultra seedy bread

This is our official house bread at mymuybueno Deli and is very popular. It's crammed with seeds so when it's sliced and toasted, they all pop and taste just amazing. Keep it well wrapped in the fridge and it will last for 5 days, and it freezes really well too. Fantastic with avocado, eggs, baked beans, nut butter, strawberry conserve, whatever you wish.

240g jumbo rolled oats
95g sunflower seeds
75g pumpkin seeds
60g flaked almonds
120g flaxseeds
4 tbsp psyllium husk
3 tbsp chia seeds
2 tsp Himalayan salt
1 tbsp maple syrup
50ml olive oil, plus extra for the tin
590ml water

For the topping

2 tbsp mixed seeds (such as pumpkin, sunflower, chia or others of your choice)

Preheat the oven to 180°c.

Place all the dry ingredients into a big bowl. Pour the liquids into another bowl or jug, then add the wet ingredients to the dry. Take your time to mix everything really well, and allow the liquid to be absorbed.

Liberally coat a 2lb loaf tin with olive oil using a silicone brush, then pour the mixture in and smooth down the top with a palette knife, ensuring all the mixture goes into each of the corners. Scatter your mixed seeds over the top then press them down firmly, otherwise when you take the loaf out they will all fall off.

Bake the bread in the oven for 55 minutes. Leave the loaf to cool in the tin for 10 minutes when done, and then run your palette knife around the loaf to ensure it comes out cleanly. Remove and leave to cool on a wire rack.

strawberry conserve

My very first recipe and the inspiration for starting mymuybueno Deli was this strawberry conserve. My original recipe won a few Great Taste Awards too, but now making it without all the refined sugar is so much better. You can use any berries in season that you wish; I also love making it with fresh figs and then jarring it up to enjoy at Christmas with a cheeseboard.

750g strawberries, hulled
5 tbsp coconut sugar
3 tbsp chia seeds
½ lemon, zested and juiced

Cut your strawberries into halves, or quarters if they are large. As this is a conserve, you want to keep the fruit in pieces to give it texture. Add the sugar, chia seeds, lemon zest and a squeeze of juice to a saucepan. Stir well.

Put the pan on a medium heat and slowly melt the sugar, then increase the temperature to get the mixture boiling for a few minutes, stirring well while it does. Now turn off the heat and leave the conserve to thicken. Once cooled, store it in the fridge for up to a week.

If you want to keep the conserve for longer, pour it into a sterilised jar then pop a wax seal on top and it will last for a few months in a cool, dark place.

This is great on toast or as a topping on any breakfast bowl, as well as a thoughtful gift to give to friends. Be careful with strawberries when not in season, as when they are fairly white, this will yield a less vibrant result.

nut butters

Making your own nut butter is so easy, delicious and more cost effective. It needs to come with a warning, because it is utterly addictive. We make all our own nut butter in mymuybueno Deli and it really makes a difference in everything from breakfast toppings to making caramels for raw desserts.

600g shelled, raw, unsalted nuts
Pinch of Himalayan salt

This recipe will work with almonds, cashews, peanuts, macadamias, pecans, pistachios and hazelnuts.

For raw nut butter (meaning you just whizz up the ingredients) follow the same steps as below without the cooking time. However, they will need a longer blending time.

Gently roasting the nuts before blending them creates a deeper flavour, and also releases the oils which help them to blend far more quickly and easily.

Preheat your oven to 150°c and place the raw nuts on a dry baking tray with a pinch of salt. Bake them for 15 to 25 minutes until golden brown. The cooking time varies depending on the nuts you are using. If using hazelnuts, leave them to cool slightly after roasting and then rub off the skins with a clean tea towel before adding to your food processor.

For a crunchy nut butter (rather than smooth) take a handful of your toasted nuts and pulse them in the food processor until crumbly, set aside and add to the butter at the end. Add the rest of the nuts to the processor and proceed as follows.

Place the nuts into your food processor and let it run. You need a good dose of patience here; it always seems like nothing is happening, but they will suddenly break down and become nut butter. Allow them to process for around 20 minutes until the mixture is completely smooth and has a runny consistency. You'll need to scrape down the bowl of the food processor every few minutes to ensure everything gets blended evenly.

Transfer the finished nut butter to a sterilised jar. Make sure you allow your nut butter to fully cool down to room temperature before putting on the lid and placing the jar in the fridge. You can store it like this for up to 3 weeks.

hazelnut chocolate spread

Once you make this yourself, you'll never go back to the store-bought product. My boys love it on toast or just on a spoon. It's so good, especially if you make the hazelnut butter yourself first. It's an extra step, but so worth it.

250g hazelnut butter (p.44)
100g maple syrup
1 tbsp coconut oil, melted
100ml almond milk
2 tbsp cacao powder
1 tsp vanilla powder

Mix the ingredients together in a blender until everything is well incorporated and smooth. Put the hazelnut chocolate spread into a sterilised jar, seal with a lid and store in the fridge for up to 3 weeks.

fresh fruit platter

SERVES 4+

It is so worth creating a fresh fruit platter. Even as a simply plated version, it's wonderful to have everyone graze from lots of delicious fruit. I love to use what's in season, chop it up and make it beautiful. I used to make these every morning for guests when I worked as a chef on super yachts, and it just stuck as something I do for my family too.

Pineapple, peeled, cored and sliced
Melon, balled or sliced
Strawberries, halved with the green tops left on
Peaches, stoned and sliced
Nectarines, stoned and sliced
Cherries, stoned and halved
Mango, peeled and sliced
Passion fruit, halved and presented upwards
Blueberries
Raspberries
Seedless grapes
Figs, quartered

Arrange whichever fruits you are using on your platter, working from the inside out to make it look colourful and beautiful. Always make sure the fruit is cold; it makes all the difference.

Serve as part of a spread, or with yoghurt and honey, or simply on its own. You could even do lunchtime versions of this with the addition of almonds, cheeses and cold cuts of meat.

pancakes

SERVES 4

These pancakes become very light and fluffy from the extra step of whisking the egg whites. It's so worthwhile to do this and really makes them heavenly. My boys love these with maple syrup and fresh berries.

110g self-raising flour
1 tsp baking powder
1 tbsp maple syrup
180ml buttermilk or Greek yoghurt
2 eggs, separated
2 tbsp butter

Place the flour, baking powder, syrup, buttermilk or yoghurt and egg yolks into a large bowl. With a wooden spoon, mix well until a nice smooth batter forms.

Next, place the egg whites into the bowl of an electric stand mixer and whisk on a high speed until stiff peaks form. Carefully fold the whisked egg whites gently into the pancake batter.

Place a large non-stick frying pan on a medium heat and add a tablespoon of butter, let it melt and wipe around the pan with a silicone brush.

Cook large pancakes one at a time, adding more butter to the pan if needed. Cook each pancake for 3 to 4 minutes until bubbles start to form, then turn the pancake over and leave for another 3 to 4 minutes on the second side until golden brown. Give the pan a wipe with kitchen paper in between batches to remove any leftover butter or residue so it doesn't burn.

Stack your pancakes on a plate and serve immediately with your topping of choice.

chia pancakes

SERVES 4

These are fantastic for those who are vegan as well as those who aren't. If I'm short on time, or have no eggs in the house, they are a go-to recipe. Great with blueberries or raspberries and maple syrup.

125g self-raising flour
1 tsp baking powder
1 tsp chia seeds
¼ tsp vanilla paste or powder
Pinch of flaked sea salt
200ml almond milk
1 tbsp maple syrup
4 tsp coconut oil, for frying

Add the flour, baking powder, chia seeds, vanilla and salt to a bowl. Add the milk and maple syrup then mix the batter well with a wooden spoon.

Place a large non-stick frying pan on a medium heat. Add two teaspoons of the coconut oil and wipe around the pan with a silicone brush.

Cook large pancakes one at a time, adding more oil to the pan if needed. Cook each pancake for 3 to 4 minutes until bubbles start to form, then turn the pancake over and leave for another 3 to 4 minutes on the second side until golden brown. Give the pan a wipe with kitchen paper in between batches to remove any leftover oil or residue so it doesn't burn.

Stack your pancakes on a plate and serve immediately with your topping of choice.

scrambled eggs with smoked salmon

SERVES 2

Scrambled eggs are such a satisfying go-to meal at any time of day, especially when accompanied by avocado, bacon, or smoked salmon. Filling and delicious, you can enjoy this with the toasted bread of your choice. I especially love it on a toasted bagel.

4 large free-range eggs
100g cream cheese
Pinch of flaked sea salt
Grind of black pepper
20g butter, plus extra for the toast
2 slices of toasted sourdough, bagels or ultra seedy bread (p.42)
4 slices of smoked salmon
1 small bunch of fresh dill, finely chopped
1 lemon, quartered

Crack your eggs into a bowl and whisk them lightly, then add the cream cheese and mix well. Season with salt and pepper.

Put your butter into a saucepan and melt over a medium heat until bubbling, then add the egg and cream cheese mixture. Stir continuously with a wooden spoon, getting right into the edges. Cook until the mixture starts to thicken up. You can then turn off the heat while the eggs are still a little runny, as the residual heat from the pan will continue to cook them.

Toast your bread of choice and slather with butter, then top with scrambled egg and two slices of smoked salmon each. Sprinkle with chopped dill, a pinch of salt and a good grind of fresh black pepper. Serve with lemon wedges.

avocado smash on toast

SERVES 1

This recipe is such a good light and quick savoury meal at any time of day. I really enjoy it topped with a soft boiled egg (p.197) to make a more substantial plateful, or even with a side of crispy bacon. In mymuybueno Deli we serve it on toasted ultra seedy bread (p.42) with plain hummus (p.72) and slow-roasted tomato which makes for a brilliant brunch or lunch.

½ medium avocado
½ tsp fresh lemon juice
⅛ tsp Himalayan salt
Grind of black pepper
1 slice of your choice of bread
½ tsp olive oil

In a small bowl, combine the avocado flesh with the lemon juice, salt and pepper. Gently mash with the back of a fork.

Toast your bread and top with the mashed avocado mixture. Drizzle with olive oil and sprinkle over your desired toppings. Any of these are great with it: flaked sea salt, chilli flakes, toasted mixed seeds or togarashi.

baked beans

SERVES 2

These are so comforting, and not just for breakfast. Filling and hearty, you just can't go wrong with a plate of beans on toast for a simple savoury breakfast or brunch option. Great on their own or with any side of your choosing, baked beans are also a perfect solution for a quick and satisfying dinner, on a jacket potato with grated cheddar cheese.

1 tbsp sunflower oil
½ onion, finely diced
1 clove of garlic, peeled and grated
1 tbsp tomato purée
1 tsp smoked paprika
¼ tsp dried thyme
1 tbsp coconut sugar
1 tbsp soy sauce
1 tsp Dijon mustard
400g tinned cannellini beans, drained and rinsed
400g passata
Grind of black pepper

Heat the oil in a saucepan, add the onion and garlic then cook over a medium heat for 5 to 8 minutes until soft and translucent. Don't skip this step, as softening the onions down is so important.

Add the tomato purée, paprika, thyme, coconut sugar, soy sauce and mustard to the pan. Cook for a couple more minutes then add the beans and passata. Simmer for at least 5 minutes, until the mixture is piping hot and the sauce has thickened a little. Season to taste with black pepper, then serve the beans however you like. Enjoy.

Drinks

hot chocolate

SERVES 1

The most delicious and comforting hot chocolate. This is also just as lovely whizzed up and served cold for children.

250ml almond or coconut milk
2 tbsp maple syrup
2 tbsp cacao powder
Pinch of ground cinnamon
Pinch of ground nutmeg
1 Medjool date, pitted
1 tbsp almond butter
Pinch of Himalayan salt

Blitz everything together in a blender and then heat the mixture in a saucepan. Finish with an electric milk frother.

spiced matcha latte

SERVES 1

I didn't convert to matcha until very recently, and I only enjoy it with my spice blend. When I've had a really long day and have consumed too much coffee, this works wonders as a pick-me-up and gentler caffeine boost. Find a really good quality ceremonial matcha for a better flavour; it's expensive but it will last. I use carton milks for this; just ensure you check they are sugar-free.

1 tsp matcha green tea powder
$1/8$ tsp ground turmeric
$1/8$ tsp ground ginger
$1/4$ tsp ground cinnamon
1 tbsp hot water
125ml almond milk
125ml carton rice milk
1 tsp maple syrup or honey (optional)

If you are using a bamboo whisk, soften the tines by soaking them in hot water. A metal whisk also works fine. Place the matcha green tea powder in a bowl with the turmeric, ginger and cinnamon. Pour the hot water over your matcha and whisk vigorously until frothy. Using a 'W' motion helps, rather than a circular one. This step will really help to make your matcha latte smooth, creamy and lump-free. Pour the spiced matcha into a mug.

Heat your milks in a saucepan until hot and use an electric milk frother to get a nice finish. Add to your mug and stir to combine.

Sweeten to taste with maple syrup or honey if you like.

golden turmeric latte

I discovered the healing powers of turmeric when our dog Hank had problems with his joints, and a friend suggested giving him a turmeric mix with his food. It worked, and my first thought was that we really need to be drinking this too. I found the flavour hard to palate, so like the matcha, I add other spices which make it more enjoyable.

250ml almond milk
1 tsp ground turmeric
1 cinnamon stick
1 cardamom pod
1 tsp maple syrup
Pinch of ground ginger
Grind of black pepper

Heat the almond milk in a saucepan on a low temperature. Add in the turmeric, cinnamon stick, cardamom pod, maple syrup, ginger and pepper and stir frequently for about 3 minutes until hot.

Remove from the heat and take out the cardamom pod and cinnamon stick. You can save these and reuse them both for another three cups.

Froth the top of the milk for a few seconds with an electric milk frother. Pour into a mug and add more maple syrup to taste if required. Stir well.

reishi chai latte

This is a nourishing 'hug in a mug' and is very popular in mymuybueno Deli during the winter months. The addition of reishi powder boosts your immune system, and I find it helps me with fatigue too. It gives it a really earthy flavour. I know some may squirm at the idea of a mushroom powder, but its savoury note balances well with all the other ingredients.

1 chai tea bag
25ml boiling water
250ml almond or coconut milk
1 tsp reishi powder
1 tsp cacao powder
1 tsp almond butter
1 tbsp maple syrup or honey
Pinch of ground cinnamon

Place the tea bag in a mug with the boiling water and leave to steep for 3 minutes, then discard the teabag. Transfer the chai tea to your blender, add all the other ingredients and blend well so that the almond butter breaks down. Transfer the mixture into a saucepan and heat well. Once hot, pour the reishi chai latte into your mug, sprinkle with cinnamon and enjoy.

smoothies

This is such a useful go-to formula that you can tweak according to your own taste and preferences. The addition of powders is always wonderful, such as adding acai to the berry one for an extra boost. I also love to do a version with peanut butter, and you can throw in oats to thicken it up, or even chia seeds for a bit of crunch.

250ml almond milk (or any other milk of your choice)
1 frozen banana, sliced
2 Medjool dates, pitted
1 tbsp almond butter

Place all the ingredients for your chosen smoothie in the blender and whizz together really well for 2 to 3 minutes. If you are using fresh spinach, ensure the leaves are especially well blended and no bits remain. Enjoy.

Green
Add 1 large handful of fresh or frozen spinach

Chocolate
Add 2 tbsp cacao powder

Berry
Add 200g mixed frozen berries
(strawberries, blueberries, blackberries)

Maca
Add ½ tsp maca powder
Pinch of ground cinnamon
Pinch of freshly grated nutmeg

wake up juice

This is my go-to 'wake me up and get me going' juice. It energises and hydrates you brilliantly to start your day with a boost. I add extra lemon and ginger when I'm feeling run down, you can adjust the ginger to your own preference. Make sure all your fruit is cold from the fridge. I quadruple this recipe to make a big jug for the whole family to enjoy.

2 Golden Delicious apples
2 large carrots
2cm fresh ginger
⅓ lemon

Remove the stem from the apples, and cut it into quarters. Remove the ends from your carrots and chop them into quarters. You don't need to peel the ginger or the lemon.

Juice the ingredients in this order: one apple, the ginger, lemon, carrots, and then the other apple. This ensures that the ginger and lemon go through between the hardy fruit and veg, and it extracts the juice properly from them.

green juice

SERVES 1

This green juice is crammed full of so much goodness, and really nourishes your body. It tastes so good that my boys have no idea just how many greens are inside. With this recipe, you extract the juice first, and then add it to your blender with the avocado which makes it filling. You can add a teaspoon of wheatgrass and/or spirulina to the blender to help it cleanse your gut too.

3 Golden Delicious apples
2cm broccoli stem
2cm courgette
1 handful of spinach or kale leaves
1 stick of celery
⅓ lime, peeled
2½cm cucumber
¼ pineapple, peeled
½ avocado
2 ice cubes

Remove the stem from the apples, and cut it into quarters.

Juice the ingredients in this order: the first two apples, broccoli stem, courgette, spinach or kale leaves, celery, lime, cucumber, pineapple and then the final apple.

When juicing leaves (like spinach or kale) always sandwich them between some hard fruit or veg, as this way they will get through the juicer properly and the juice will be extracted well.

Add your juice to your blender. Scoop out the avocado flesh and blend it with the ice and juice. If you are adding powders such as spirulina or wheatgrass they should also go in now.

beet-i-full juice

SERVES 1

This one is really delicious and leaves you very satisfied; my boys absolutely love it. We demolish this juice within minutes of making it. You can throw any extra raw veg in there too without drastically changing the result. It's such a good way to give your body a huge plate of fruit and vegetables that you would never sit and eat whole, plus the colour is sensational.

2 Golden Delicious apples

1 carrot

½ stick of celery

Large handful of spinach or kale leaves

¼ cucumber

2cm broccoli stem

1 medium raw beetroot

2cm courgette

⅓ lemon

2cm fresh ginger

⅛ pineapple, peeled

Remove the stem from the apples, and cut them into quarters. Remove the ends from your carrot and chop it into quarters. Ensure your fruit and veg is cold; it makes all the difference.

When juicing leaves (like spinach or kale) always sandwich them between some hard fruit or veg, as this way they will get through the juicer properly and the juice will be extracted well.

Juice the ingredients in this order: your first apple, carrot, celery, spinach or kale leaves, cucumber, broccoli, beetroot, courgette, lemon, ginger, pineapple, and the final apple. Enjoy.

Breaking bread together

Living in Spain has definitely influenced my love of tapas-style eating, but it is as a mother that my passion for this type of food was cemented. Not only is it time saving, but it brings people together through a love of good food and the enjoyment of eating it together.

Everyone gets to have a little of everything, and they can easily and frequently go back for more, which everyone often does, meaning my children tend to eat more as a result. It also means conversation can flow, as we take turns dishing up for one another, talking about our days and the food we are eating.

As my husband Paul has said, this book is my greatest hits, and it really is. It's all the good food I've been making for years. Many recipes are the dishes I used to cook for the crew when working as a chef on super yachts, and some even for the guests. Even the most famous people in the world don't always want high-end plated food, and dishes like my Thai green chicken curry or pesto and Parmesan salmon have always been popular favourites. They are now the very same dishes I make to feed my family and myself at home, and I'm certain you'll enjoy eating them just as much as we do.

Trying to create some slower moments, to enjoy some quality time on your own making good food for yourself, your family or friends.

Time, once again, is always an issue. Life is busy. It seems that we are busier now than we have ever been before, or that the generations before us could ever have imagined. The instantaneousness of the digital world we live in means we are constantly delivering to the expectations all around us; we put so much pressure on ourselves, but often we put ourselves last.

Trying to create some slower moments, to enjoy some quality time on your own making good food for yourself, your family or friends, and to sit and enjoy that food together, is key to having real quality time to nourish yourself in mind, body and soul.

I encourage you to mix and match dishes from each of these next chapters together.

The next chapter covers what I like to call 'pickies' with all my savoury bites. Sometimes I have little time and will just make some hummus or guacamole with baked tortilla chips, and then add some cold cuts and cheeses, hard boiled eggs, olives, anchovies and cherry tomatoes to pad it out for a great lunch or dinner. With more planning and a little more time, you can make a bigger spread, or just serve a big platter of coconut panko prawns on their own.

I encourage you to mix and match dishes from each of these next chapters together. I've shown you a few options for a Thai (p.86), Moroccan (p.140) and also an Indian spread (p.108) to inspire you.

Making big batches of different dishes, such as the quinoa, couscous or hummus, means you have something ready in the fridge and then only need to do something easy, such as roast some vegetables or salmon to go with it. Other days you may fancy a hearty bowl of goodness. I love spicy food, so I've

included a few curries and also soupy broths with noodles like the laksa and ramen, which are quick, easy and so tasty. Making stews is another fantastic and easy way to warm up your day, simply throwing everything into a pot and into the oven, and letting it do its job while you can do other things, knowing you'll have a bowl of goodness to look forward to in a matter of hours.

It's all about balance and moderation, and the enjoyment that comes from cooking and sharing this food with others.

I love a big family meal of a traditional British roast dinner with all the trimmings, so have included recipes over the next chapters that enable you to put together a fabulous roast beef or chicken with roast potatoes, honey glazed carrots and other delicious vegetables, plus my gravy. But you could also make my garlic butter chicken and serve it with hummus and roasted Mediterranean veg, flatbreads and couscous, for a totally different meal. Often I have leftovers too, which then means lunch or dinner is already done for the next day.

Getting the most out of cooking and eating well each day is all about time management. Some days making a quick and easy soup works, and will feed everyone well. Other days you'll plan ahead and make a few dishes, or you may have guests coming over for which making something like the paella will be a real winner.

I've made many of my recipes easily adaptable, so if you're vegan, vegetarian or gluten-free, you can very easily swap out the meat and fish for veg, omit fish sauce, or use gluten-free flour. Simple swaps such as Greek yoghurt for coconut yoghurt make my recipes accessible to everyone.

Some days you can be much healthier with juicing and salads, other days you may really want to indulge in a pizza or a big roast. It's all about balance and moderation, and the enjoyment that comes from cooking and sharing this food with others.

Savoury Bites

plain and beetroot hummus

SERVES 4

I could eat hummus all day long: it's creamy, it's moreish, it's delicious. We eat a lot of hummus in our house, simply with carrot sticks, baked tortilla chips or flatbreads and as a side with a Moroccan style feast (p.140). Roasting the garlic first mellows and sweetens it.

400g tinned chickpeas, drained and rinsed
2 tbsp tahini
1 clove of garlic, peeled
1 tbsp lemon juice
2 tbsp olive oil
3 tbsp water
1 tsp ground cumin
Pinch of flaked sea salt
Grind of black pepper

For the beetroot hummus
200g cooked beetroot, drained and chopped

For the plain hummus

Preheat your oven to 180°c. Place your garlic on a tray or inside some foil and roast for 10 minutes.

Place the chickpeas, tahini, roasted garlic, lemon juice, olive oil, water, cumin, salt and pepper in a food processor then blend until smooth.

For the beetroot hummus

Follow the above method but use half the amount of tahini and ground cumin, leave out the water and add the beetroot. Blend all the ingredients together in a food processor as above.

flatbreads

MAKES 6 LARGE OR 12 SMALL

These are so quick and versatile. You can serve them with hummus, grilled meat, fish, vegetables and curries, or you could even top them with tomato sauce and cheese to grill for mega-fast pizzas.

300g self-raising flour, plus extra for dusting
1 tsp baking powder
2 tsp flaked sea salt
300g Greek or coconut yoghurt
1 tbsp olive oil

For the topping (optional)
30g salted butter, melted, or olive oil
Handful of fresh coriander leaves, chopped

In a large bowl, mix the flour, baking powder and salt together well. Add the yoghurt and olive oil and mix thoroughly with a spoon until it all comes together to form a dough, which should be quite sticky.

Dust a clean work surface with flour, turn the dough out onto it and knead for a few minutes. Place the dough back into the bowl and cover with a damp tea towel, then leave for 20 minutes to rest.

Again, dust your work surface and rolling pin with flour, then divide the rested dough in half, then divide each half into three or six equal pieces, depending on whether you are making them large or small.

With your hands, gently pat the dough to flatten it out, then use a rolling pin to roll each piece into your flatbreads.

Place a griddle over a high heat and, once hot, lay your first flatbread into the dry pan. Cook for around 1 minute without moving, then turn it over using tongs and cook for 1 minute on the other side. Ensure the dough is cooked through with nice charred lines. Transfer the cooked flatbread to a warm plate.

Repeat with the remaining flatbreads, then, if using, brush with the melted butter or olive oil and scatter with chopped coriander.

guacamole

Amazing as a dip with baked tortilla chips. You can omit the chilli to make it child-friendly,
or if you aren't a huge fan of spice.

1 small red onion, finely chopped
1 fresh red bird's eye chilli, finely chopped
1 large ripe tomato, finely chopped
3 ripe avocados (not bruised)
Handful of fresh coriander leaves, roughly chopped
1 lime, juiced
1 tbsp olive oil
½ tsp flaked sea salt
Grind of black pepper

Mix your chopped onion, chilli and tomato together in a bowl. Roughly chop the avocado flesh into 1cm cubes and add them to the bowl with the coriander, lime juice, olive oil, salt and pepper.

Using the back of a fork, mash around half the avocado and then continue to mix all the ingredients together well. Add more lime juice or salt to taste before serving.

baked tortilla chips

Really simple and very effective, these are great with hummus and guacamole. You can also sprinkle on paprika,
cumin or cayenne with the salt for different flavours and to enjoy as a snack all on their own.

8 flour or corn tortillas
1 tbsp sunflower oil
1 tsp salt

Preheat your oven to 180°c.

Cut each tortilla into eight triangular wedges and arrange them in a single layer on a baking tray.

Put some sunflower oil into a bowl and lightly brush some onto each triangle.

Sprinkle a little salt onto the tortillas and then bake them for 8 to 12 minutes until just golden. Keep a close eye on them; I've burnt too many trays before when distracted.

Leave them to crisp up and cool slightly before eating.

spinach and feta frittata

SERVES 4

Frittatas are such quick and easy bites to have at any time of day. I love making and serving them cold for a picnic, as well as a mid-morning dish or even a light dinner. It is really great with goat's cheese as well as tomatoes or olives, or even roasted vegetables.

6 eggs, beaten
4 tbsp cream
Fresh dill, roughly chopped
Pinch of flaked sea salt
Grind of black pepper
1 tbsp sunflower oil
½ red onion, peeled and sliced
Large handful of baby spinach
100g feta, cut into 1cm cubes

Preheat the oven to 180°c.

In a bowl, mix the beaten eggs with the cream, dill, salt and pepper and set aside.

Next, add the oil to a medium ovenproof frying pan, place it over a medium heat, then add the onion and cook for 3 minutes until starting to soften.

Add the spinach to the pan and stir until it starts to wilt, then add the feta cubes.

Pour your egg mixture over the ingredients in the pan and gently stir everything together so it is all well distributed. Allow the frittata to cook on the hob for 1 minute until you see the edges start to firm up.

Place it into the preheated oven for 20 minutes, or until just set in the centre.

Remove the pan from the oven and leave to cool for a few minutes. Using gloves on the hot handle, turn it upside down to transfer the frittata onto a board or alternatively serve it straight from the pan. Cut into wedges, season again and then serve, or leave the frittata to cool and refrigerate until needed.

prawn and chive gyoza

MAKES 24

This is a simple recipe to satisfy the need for delicious dumplings. Chopping rather than mincing the prawns adds texture to the filling. The pleating of the dumplings takes just a little time, but be patient and remember they don't need to be perfect. When making a large batch, I freeze half before cooking so there's more to enjoy another time.

For the gyoza dipping sauce

See recipe on page 191

For the gyoza

500g raw large prawns, peeled, deveined and finely chopped

3 cloves of garlic, grated

1 tbsp fresh chives, finely chopped

1 red bird's eye chilli, finely chopped

2 tbsp soy sauce

2 tsp sesame oil

24 gyoza wrappers

For frying

1 tbsp sunflower oil

1 tsp sesame oil

Make the dipping sauce first, and leave the flavours to develop while you make the gyoza.

For the gyoza

Mix the chopped prawns with the garlic, chives, chilli, soy sauce and sesame oil.

Place the gyoza wrappers on a flat surface. Spoon one heaped teaspoon of the filling into the centre of each wrapper, then brush the edges with cold water. Bring the edges of the wrapper together, pinching gently to create pleats, and press together to seal. Repeat with the remaining wrappers and prawn mixture.

To steam the gyoza

Place a steamer lined with parchment paper over a saucepan of simmering water. Cook the dumplings, in small batches, for 12 to 14 minutes or until tender and cooked through. Serve immediately and enjoy with your dipping sauce.

To fry the gyoza

Add the tablespoon of sunflower oil to a frying pan over a medium heat. When the pan is hot, place the gyoza in a single layer, flat side down and cook for around 3 minutes until the bottom of the gyoza turns golden brown. Add 100ml of water to the pan. Immediately cover with a lid or foil, and steam the gyoza this way for 3 minutes or until most of the water evaporates. Remove the lid to evaporate any remaining water. Drizzle the sesame oil around the frying pan to finish. Serve immediately and enjoy with your dipping sauce.

coconut panko prawns

SERVES 4

These are hugely popular and taste so good, well worth the extra effort and a little mess. I make a big pile and they are always demolished in record time, just a massive hit with everyone. You can also use oyster mushrooms or cauliflower too instead of the prawns, and I've added a vegan batter below.

200g plain flour
1 tsp baking powder
Pinch of flaked sea salt
Grind of black pepper
1 egg, beaten
140ml ice cold water
50g panko breadcrumbs
50g desiccated coconut
500g raw king prawns, peeled and deveined with tails left on
300ml sunflower oil, for frying
1 lime, cut into wedges

To make the batter, sift 150g of the flour into a bowl with the baking powder and salt. Make a well in the centre and break in the egg. Whisk in the cold water to make a smooth batter.

For a vegan option, replace the egg with a tablespoon of apple cider vinegar and the water with almond milk.

Put the remaining flour into a separate bowl and season generously with salt and pepper. In a separate bowl, combine the panko breadcrumbs and desiccated coconut.

You now have a production line set up of three different bowls. It helps if you have them in the right order from left to right: flour, batter and then the coconut panko mix.

Holding your raw prawn by the tail, dredge it in the seasoned flour to coat the whole body. Shake off any excess and then dunk it carefully into the batter. Again, gently shake off any excess, then roll the prawn in the panko mix, carefully pressing down to ensure the breadcrumbs stick well all over.

Put the prawn on a lined tray and repeat until all the prawns are coated, leaving space between each one. You will end up with 'Incredible Hulk' fingers by the end of it with all the flour, batter and crumbs stuck to them.

Pour approximately 3cm of sunflower oil into a large deep frying pan and place on a medium heat.

In batches, using a slotted spoon, carefully lower the prawns into the hot oil and fry for 1 to 2 minutes until golden and crisp on all sides. Do not overcrowd the pan because the oil will rise up and must not overflow. Transfer the cooked prawns to a plate lined with plenty of kitchen paper to absorb the oil. Repeat the process until all the coated prawns are cooked. Serve with lime wedges.

chicken satays

SERVES 4

Satays are a firm favourite in our house, either as a big platter to share, or even as a lunch or dinner served with coconut rice and a Thai green salad. You can also use king prawns, beef, cauliflower or mushrooms.

4 chicken breasts

For the marinade
Small piece of fresh ginger
1 clove of garlic
1 lime, juiced
1 tbsp soy sauce
1 tbsp runny honey
1 tsp peanut butter

For the satay sauce
See recipe on page 191

To serve
Fresh coriander leaves
Chopped peanuts
Lime wedges

Soak 20 small wooden skewers in water for about half an hour, and preheat the oven to 180°c.

To make the marinade, peel and grate the ginger and garlic then place them in a bowl along with the lime juice, soy sauce, honey and peanut butter. Mix everything together well.

Place the chicken breasts into a sealable bag and bash with a rolling pin until they are flattened. Be careful not to hit them too hard, so you don't make any holes or tears in the chicken. Remove and slice up the chicken then put the strips back into the bag with the marinade while you make the dipping sauce. If you have time, you can do this step earlier in the day, or the day before, and leave the chicken in the fridge to marinate well.

Thread the marinated chicken strips onto the soaked skewers in an S shape so they are held on at three points. Place them on a lined baking tray and cook for 12 minutes in the preheated oven, or until the chicken is cooked through. Serve with the satay dipping sauce and fresh coriander, chopped peanuts and lime wedges.

rainbow rolls

These are fiddly to start with, but take your time with them and use my tips in the method below to help you make perfect rolls every time. You can choose any selection of fillings.

8 rice paper wrappers

For the fillings

Fresh mint leaves

Fresh coriander leaves

16 prawns, cooked and peeled

5 gem lettuce leaves, thinly sliced

1 medium carrot, peeled and cut into matchsticks

1 red bell pepper, deseeded and cut into matchsticks

½ cucumber, deseeded and cut into matchsticks

4 radishes, thinly sliced

1 raw beetroot, grated

1 avocado, thinly sliced

1 mango, thinly sliced

For the almond butter dipping sauce

See recipe on page 191

Half fill a large frying pan with cold water. I like to use a frying pan as it's the perfect size and depth, but a wide bowl would work too. Submerge the first rice paper sheet for 30 seconds or until softened, then place on a damp tea towel laid out on a clean work surface.

For the fillings

Gently smooth out the first wrap into a circle. Be careful as once wet, they are very fragile and can break easily. Place a few mint and coriander leaves in a single layer in the centre of the sheet, leaving space on each side. Add two prawns, facing the same way, then a pile of sliced vegetables of your choice, and some mango to the lower half of the sheet. Fold in the sides and roll up to enclose the filling.

Repeat the process for all eight rolls, keeping your assembled rolls covered with a damp tea towel. These can be prepared an hour or two in advance, just keep them in the fridge with the damp tea towel and then cling film over the top so they don't dry out.

Serve your rainbow rolls with the almond butter dipping sauce. Enjoy.

thai green
chicken curry
p.98

chicken satays
p.83
satay dipping sauce
p.191

spicy green
papaya salad
p.158

coconut rice
p.197

coconut panko prawns
p.82

gyoza dipping sauce
p.191

calamari

SERVES 4

Don't be scared of squid. The hardest part, and the most tedious, is cleaning it, but it's worth your while
because calamari is so delicious and great for sharing.

4 whole large squid with tentacles
300ml sunflower oil, for frying
1 lemon, zested
100g plain flour
Pinch of flaked sea salt
Grind of black pepper
1 lemon, cut into wedges

To prepare the squid, first remove the tentacles by pulling them away from the body. Set aside. The head and the ink sac should come out relatively easily when pulled, along with the clear quill that is inside. It looks like a long piece of plastic. The flaps, or wings as they are also known, now need to be removed along with the purple skin. Peel it all off, and then rinse the entire squid under cold running water.

Pat your prepared squid dry with kitchen paper. Slice the tubes horizontally into rings.

Pour approximately 3cm of sunflower oil into a large deep frying pan and place on a medium heat.

Place the squid rings and tentacles on a large plate. Sprinkle over the lemon zest then squeeze over most of the juice. Mix well.

Place the flour into a bowl with a good pinch of salt and pepper, then add the squid and toss to coat. Do this in a few batches until all your squid is coated.

Once the oil is hot enough, in batches, using a slotted spoon, carefully lower the squid into the hot oil and fry for 3 to 4 minutes, or until golden and crisp on the outside and cooked through. Transfer to a plate lined with plenty of kitchen paper to absorb the oil. Repeat the process with the rest of the coated squid.

Serve with wedges of lemon and aioli (p.190) I added a pinch of saffron to mine here.

sushi

I adore sushi, and it is actually far simpler to make than you think. I like to make these simple maki rolls. They are great for lunch, an evening meal, or a simple snack. You could even wrap them whole in greaseproof paper to take on a picnic. I love making them with my boys and we enjoy filling them and rolling together. You can add any fillings you wish.

400g sushi rice
750ml cold water
2 tbsp rice vinegar
4 sheets of nori seaweed
100g fresh good quality salmon
50g cream cheese
½ cucumber, thinly sliced lengthways
1 avocado, thinly sliced lengthways

To make the rice

Rinse the sushi rice in a sieve under cold running water. Then place the clean rice into a medium saucepan with the fresh cold water. Leave it to soak for 30 minutes, then turn on the heat. Bring to the boil then immediately reduce the heat to low, cover and cook for 10 minutes until the water has been absorbed. Stir to ensure the rice isn't sticking to the pan. Remove from the heat and leave the lid on for a further 5 minutes to ensure it is cooked.

Using a silicone spatula, loosely spread the rice out on a large tray without squashing it. Drizzle the rice vinegar evenly over the warm rice and use the spatula to gently stir it in. Leave the rice to cool completely.

To fill your sushi

Put a small bowl of iced water next to you for wetting your hands continuously, so the rice doesn't stick as you work. Holding your nori sheet horizontally, cut a quarter off the top with scissors. I find this helps to form a better roll and the rest of the nori is excess that is not needed. Place your trimmed nori sheet on a bamboo sushi rolling mat, with the edge of the sheet meeting the edge of the mat closest to you.

Evenly spread some rice over the sheet to form a layer about 2mm deep, leaving 2cm of space at the top. Do not push your rice down or load it up too much. Add your fillings of choice in a horizontal line across the rice, about 1cm up from the edge closest to you.

To roll your sushi

Lift the bamboo mat and start rolling. Work from the middle, as opposed to the edges, to roll the nori sheet over the contents, keeping the filling in place with your fingers. Roll firmly but not too hard until your nearest edge meets the empty space on the other side.

Wet your finger and run some water along the clear edge, then continue rolling to stick the ends together. Press gently with your fingers to close the roll, then cut into 6 to 8 even pieces with a sharp knife, discarding (eating) the end pieces.

Repeat the filling and rolling process to use all the nori sheets. Enjoy your sushi with soy sauce, pickled ginger and wasabi. Chopsticks are of course essential.

samosas

SERVES 4

If I make these for my boys, I tone down or completely remove the chilli and garam masala. Samosas are fantastic snacks, and they also freeze really well before baking. These are great served with my tamarind dipping sauce (p.193).

400g potatoes
250g cauliflower
125g frozen peas
2 tbsp sunflower oil
1 onion, finely chopped
1 tsp cumin seeds
2 cloves of garlic, peeled and chopped
5cm fresh ginger, peeled and chopped
½–1 green bird's eye chilli to taste, finely chopped
½ tsp fennel seeds
1 tsp garam masala
1 tsp ground coriander
½ lemon, juiced
Pinch of flaked sea salt
Grind of black pepper
Handful of fresh coriander, finely chopped
1 pack of ready-made filo pastry
3-4 tbsp coconut oil, melted
2 tbsp nigella seeds

To make the filling

Peel and chop the potatoes into roughly 2½cm chunks, then chop the cauliflower into florets of a similar size. Cook the potatoes in a large pan of boiling salted water for 10 to 12 minutes, or until tender. Add the cauliflower after 3 minutes and then the frozen peas for the final minute. Drain the cooked vegetables and leave them to steam dry in the pan off the heat.

Put the sunflower oil into a large non-stick frying pan over a medium heat, add the onion and cumin seeds then cook for around 5 minutes to soften. Stir in the garlic, ginger and chilli, then fry for a further few minutes.

Bash the fennel seeds to a fine powder using a pestle and mortar, then add to the pan along with the garam masala and ground coriander. Stir well.

Stir the cooked veg into the mixture and crush gently with a potato masher, but not too much so you still have a good chunky texture. Squeeze in the lemon juice and season the filling to taste with salt and pepper. Leave it to cool, then stir through the chopped coriander.

To make the samosa

Preheat your oven to 180°c.

Unroll the filo pastry carefully, as it's very fragile, and cover with a damp tea towel. Peel off one sheet and keep the rest covered so that it doesn't dry out.

Fold one third of the pastry lengthways in towards the middle. Brush the uppermost side with melted coconut oil and fold in the other side to make a long triple-layered rectangle strip.

Place two teaspoons of the filling at one end of the strip, leaving a 2cm border. Take the right hand corner and fold diagonally to the left, enclosing the filling and forming a triangle. Fold again along the upper crease of the triangle. Keep folding in this way until you reach the end of the strip.

Place the finished samosa onto a lined baking tray and cover with a damp tea towel while you make the rest. Once finished, brush the tops of the samosa lightly with coconut oil. Sprinkle each one with nigella seeds, then bake in the centre of the oven at 180°c for 30 minutes, or until golden and crisp.

melon and jamon balls

SERVES 4

Perfect as part of a platter, a fab canapé if entertaining, or just a simple snack for everyone at any time. The combination of salty Serrano ham with the sweet cold melon is always a winner.

10 thin slices of Serrano ham
1 melon, such as cantaloupe

Cut the slices of Serrano ham in half lengthways, then fold each piece up loosely in a concertina.

Make sure the melon is cold from the fridge, then halve and deseed it. Using a melon baller, scoop out 20 balls from the melon flesh.

Pop a concertina of Serrano ham on top of each melon ball and secure with a toothpick down the middle, which will make the melon balls easier to pick up and eat. Enjoy.

courgette and feta fritters

SERVES 4

These are amazing. Once you master the steps of carefully frying them, you'll make these again and again. They're a real crowd pleaser.

500g courgette, coarsely grated
1 tsp flaked sea salt
1 small red onion, finely sliced
2 cloves of garlic, peeled and grated
1 lemon, zested
20g Parmesan block, grated
20g fresh mint, leaves chopped
1 red bird's eye chilli, finely chopped
60g self-raising flour
2 eggs, lightly beaten
Grind of black pepper
150g feta, broken into 1-2cm chunks
300ml sunflower oil, for frying
1 lemon, cut into wedges

Place the grated courgette into a colander and sprinkle over the salt. Set aside for 10 minutes, then squeeze to remove most of the liquid.

Transfer the prepared courgette to a large bowl and add the onion, garlic, lemon zest, Parmesan, mint, chilli, flour, eggs and black pepper. Mix well to form a uniform batter, then fold in the feta cheese.

Pour approximately 3cm of sunflower oil into a large deep frying pan and place on a medium heat.

Once the oil is hot enough, carefully drop two heaped tablespoons of the mixture into the pan, spacing them well apart. Use the spoons to squeeze each spoonful together first, to help remove any excess liquid and form an oval shape. Cook for 5 minutes, turning once halfway through, until golden and crisp on both sides. Transfer to a plate lined with plenty of kitchen paper to absorb the oil. Repeat the process until all your mixture is used up.

If your oil starts to get too full of little bits that have broken off the fritters, these will burn so stop frying, carefully remove all of these with a slotted spoon, and then continue.

Serve the courgette and feta fritters with lemon wedges to squeeze over. I like these served with chilli tomato chutney (p.195) and crème fraîche.

Hearty Bowls

thai green chicken curry

SERVES 6

I am obsessed with Thai curry. I went on an amazing trip to Thailand many years ago to train in Thai cuisine, and I learnt so much. My boys love this; for them I use just a touch of paste and extra coconut milk along with sliced carrots and peas. You can remove the chicken and use prawns or extra vegetables instead; aubergine works well.

For the paste

2 cloves of garlic

3 shallots

30g fresh ginger or galangal

2 lemongrass stalks (white part only)

4 green bird's eye chillies

6 kaffir lime leaves, chopped

Handful of fresh coriander

1 tbsp palm sugar, grated

½ tsp shrimp paste

2 tbsp coconut oil

1 tsp ground cumin

2 tsp ground coriander

For the curry

800g skinless chicken thighs

3 tbsp coconut oil

300g shiitake mushrooms

800ml tinned coconut milk, shaken well before opening

3 kaffir lime leaves, stems removed, thinly sliced

2 tbsp fish sauce

200g mangetout

Handful of fresh Thai basil leaves

Handful of fresh coriander leaves

2 limes

For the paste

Peel and chop the garlic, shallots and ginger or galangal then place them into a food processor. Trim the ends off the lemongrass, remove the tough outer leaves, then chop the white part and add it to the processor. Trim and add the chillies along with the kaffir lime leaves, coriander, palm sugar, shrimp paste, coconut oil and ground cumin and coriander. Blitz the mixture really well; you will need to stop and push the paste from the sides down into the machine and go again until it's blended well.

For the curry

Slice the chicken into 2cm pieces and heat one tablespoon of the coconut oil in a large frying pan on a medium heat. Add the chicken and fry until golden brown and mostly cooked. Set aside.

In the same pan, heat another spoonful of coconut oil and fry the mushrooms for 5 minutes until cooked. If they start to stick just add a little more oil and keep them moving round the pan. Add to the same plate as your chicken.

In a large separate saucepan over a medium heat, add a tablespoon of coconut oil, then add two tablespoons of your Thai green curry paste and cook for just a minute. Pour in the coconut milk, stir well and simmer for 5 minutes. At this stage, taste the sauce. If you would like it to have more of a kick, add a touch more paste, if it's too spicy for you, add more coconut milk. Freeze your remaining paste in a sealable bag.

Add the chicken, mushrooms and sliced kaffir lime leaves to the saucepan, then reduce the heat to low and cook for a further 5 minutes, or until the chicken is cooked through. Add the fish sauce, mangetout and Thai basil in the final minute as you want the mangetout to only just cook so it's still crunchy. The basil leaves will enhance the dish with the hint of aniseed they carry.

Serve your curry with chopped fresh coriander, extra Thai basil, lime wedges and plain or coconut rice (p.197). Enjoy.

chicken tikka masala

SERVES 6

A really good masala is sometimes just the ticket after a long day. In mymuybueno Deli
we use roasted cauliflower instead of the chicken; it's really popular.

For the paste

2 tsp each of ground cumin, coriander,
smoked paprika and garam masala

1 tsp each of cayenne pepper
and ground turmeric

3 cardamom pods

3 cloves of garlic, peeled and roughly chopped

1 shallot, peeled and roughly chopped

2 red bird's eye chillies, roughly chopped

2cm fresh ginger, peeled and chopped

1 tbsp tomato purée

Handful of fresh coriander

2 tbsp ground almonds

2 tbsp sunflower oil

1 tbsp water

For the curry

4 tbsp sunflower oil

1 large onion, sliced

1 clove of garlic, peeled and sliced

Pinch of flaked sea salt

Grind of black pepper

400g tinned chopped tomatoes

2 tbsp tomato purée

400ml tinned coconut milk, shaken well
before opening

8 boneless and skinless chicken thighs

Chopped coriander leaves, to garnish

For the paste

Toast all the spices in a dry pan, then add to your food processor with all the remaining ingredients and blitz until the paste comes together. Add a tablespoon of water if needed.

For the curry

Heat half of the oil in a large saucepan over a medium-high heat, add the onion and garlic and cook for a few minutes until softened and translucent.

Season with salt and black pepper, add the tomatoes, purée, all your paste and the coconut milk, then bring to the boil. Turn the heat down to low, cover with a lid and simmer for 10 minutes. At this stage, taste the sauce. If it's too spicy for you, add more coconut milk.

Slice the chicken into small 2cm pieces and heat one tablespoon of oil in a large frying pan on a medium heat. Add the chicken and fry until golden brown and almost cooked. Then add the chicken to the curry and simmer for another 10 minutes until the chicken is cooked through. Serve with fresh coriander scattered over the top and plain rice and flatbreads on the side (p.72).

lentil dahl

Spicy and comforting, this is simply perfect on its own or enjoyed with rice, flatbreads and pineapple chutney. It's also great served as a side with an Indian style spread (p.108).

2 tbsp coconut oil

1 tsp each of cumin seeds and mustard seeds

1 onion, finely diced

2 cloves of garlic, peeled and finely chopped

2 red bird's eye chillies, finely chopped

1 tsp fresh ginger, peeled and grated

1 large tomato, finely chopped

2 tbsp coriander stalks, finely chopped

1 tsp each of ground coriander, cumin, cinnamon, turmeric, curry powder and dried chilli flakes

350g dried green lentils

400ml vegetable stock

800ml tinned coconut milk, shaken well before opening

Pinch of flaked sea salt

Squeeze of lemon juice

100g fresh coriander leaves, chopped

Place a large pan over a medium heat, melt the coconut oil in it then cook the cumin and mustard seeds for a minute until fragrant and starting to pop.

Add the onion, garlic, chilli, ginger, tomato and coriander stalks to the seeds and cook until the onions and garlic start to soften, then add all the remaining dry spices and mix well.

Stir in the lentils, vegetable stock and half of the coconut milk. When it all starts bubbling, reduce the heat to low and cook the dahl for 2 hours with the lid on, checking on it often and stirring to ensure that it doesn't stick to the bottom. If it starts to stick or looks like it's drying out, add up to 200ml of water.

Once the lentils are cooked, add the remaining coconut milk and stir through the dahl to make it really creamy. Add salt to taste at the very end of the cooking process (any earlier will make the lentils toughen up). Add a squeeze of lemon juice then serve with the fresh coriander, rice or flatbreads and pineapple chutney (p.195).

massaman curry

SERVES 6

This curry is just so good. The paste for this recipe requires a little more effort, but you will have enough left to freeze for another day. You can use other cuts of beef, but for this curry I find that cheeks provide that absolute melt-in-your-mouth texture once slow cooked. To make this plant-based, I use tinned organic green jackfruit and cook just until the potato and jackfruit are tender.

For the paste

5 large finger-length dried chillies, submerged in water

5 cloves

5 cardamom pods

1 tbsp each coriander seeds and cumin seeds

1 cinnamon stick

1 star anise

1 fresh bay leaf

1 tsp flaked sea salt

1 tbsp coconut oil

4cm fresh galangal or ginger, peeled and roughly chopped

4 lemongrass stalks, finely chopped (white part only)

5 shallots, peeled and sliced

5 cloves of garlic, peeled and sliced

1 tsp shrimp paste

2 kaffir lime leaves

4 tbsp coriander stalks

2 tbsp desiccated coconut

1 tbsp peanuts

½ tsp whole nutmeg, grated

1 tbsp fish sauce

For the curry

2 tbsp sunflower oil

1kg beef cheeks (approx. 3 large ones), cut into 3cm dice

1 large onion, halved and finely sliced

800ml tinned coconut milk, shaken well before opening

500ml beef stock

1 large potato, cut into 2cm cubes

1 tbsp palm sugar, grated

1 tbsp fish sauce

2 tbsp peanuts, toasted and crushed

For the paste

In a dry pan, combine the soaked chillies, cloves, cardamom pods, coriander and cumin seeds, cinnamon stick, star anise, bay leaf and salt. Toast until fragrant then transfer the spices into a food processor and blitz to a fine powder.

Add the coconut oil to a non-stick frying pan over a medium heat, and cook the galangal or ginger, lemongrass, shallots, garlic and shrimp paste for 1 to 2 minutes. Remove from the heat and leave to cool.

Add the lemongrass mixture to your food processor along with the toasted ground spices and the lime leaves, coriander stalks, coconut, peanuts, nutmeg, fish sauce and three tablespoons of water. Blitz up well, for a good minute.

For the curry

Preheat the oven to 160°c. Put your pan back on a high heat with half of the sunflower oil and add the diced beef cheek, working quickly with tongs to turn all the cubes so they seal and brown all over. Transfer them to a plate and set aside.

Add the remaining sunflower oil to a casserole dish over a medium heat and add the sliced onion with half of your paste. Stir well and cook for 1 to 2 minutes. As it starts to cook, add half of the coconut milk and mix well.

Add the beef stock and the beef cheeks into the casserole dish on the hob and bring to the boil, then reduce the heat and simmer for 10 minutes. Place into the oven for 1 hour with the lid on.

Remove from the oven. At this stage, taste the curry. If you would like it to have more of a kick, add a touch more paste, if it's too spicy, add more coconut milk. Freeze your remaining paste in a sealable bag.

Place the casserole dish back into the oven and cook for a second hour, then remove to stir it and add the remaining coconut milk, the potato, palm sugar and fish sauce. Cook for a third and final hour. As the potato cooks, it will break down and help to thicken the curry.

Once it has had 3 hours, stir well and check that the beef cheeks are melt-in-your-mouth soft.

If the curry looks too wet, pop it back into the oven for 30 minutes. If it's drying out at any point, add a little more water. Serve with plain rice (p.197) and top with the toasted and crushed peanuts.

chickpea and sweet potato curry

SERVES 6

Rich and creamy, hearty and full of flavour. With extra coconut milk, my boys will happily lap up a big bowl of this.
Omit the fish sauce for a vegan curry.

½ tsp each of ground turmeric, paprika,
garam masala, cinnamon and chilli powder

1 tsp curry powder

3 large sweet potatoes

Pinch of flaked sea salt

3 tbsp coconut oil, melted

1 tsp each of cumin seeds and mustard seeds

2 cloves of garlic, peeled and sliced

1 large red onion, halved and sliced

2 green bird's eye chillies, sliced

2cm fresh ginger, peeled and grated

Handful of fresh coriander, leaves and stalks,
finely chopped

400g tinned chickpeas, drained and rinsed

200g tinned chopped tomatoes

800ml tinned coconut milk, shaken well
before opening

1 tbsp fish sauce

100g spinach leaves

Grind of black pepper

Fresh coriander, roughly chopped

Preheat the oven to 220°c.

In a bowl, mix the turmeric, paprika, garam masala, cinnamon, chilli powder and curry powder.

Peel the sweet potatoes then chop them into 2cm chunks. Place them on a baking tray with the salt, two tablespoons of the melted coconut oil and the spice blend. Roast in the preheated oven for 30 minutes until the sweet potato is cooked through and browned nicely; the spices will have toasted and been absorbed well. Cooking the potato this way helps to retain its integrity.

In a large saucepan over a medium heat, cook the cumin and mustard seeds in the remaining tablespoon of coconut oil for 1 minute until they release their fragrance and start to pop. Add the sliced garlic and onion to the pan and cook for 3 minutes until soft until soft and translucent.

Add the chillies, ginger, fresh coriander and chickpeas to the pan, then cook for just a minute, add the tomatoes, then cover and cook for 10 minutes.

Next add the coconut milk, fish sauce and the roasted sweet potatoes to the pot and stir well. Cook for a few minutes just to ensure any bite left in the potato is cooked out.

Stir in the spinach and cook until wilted, season with salt and pepper to taste, then serve the curry scattered with fresh coriander, alongside plain or coconut rice (p.197) and raita (p.191).

samosas
p.92
tamarind
dipping sauce
p.193

raita
p.191

massaman curry
p.104

lentil dahl
p.102

chickpea
and sweet
potato curry
p.106

flatbreads
p.72

pineapple
chutney
p.195

plain rice
p.197

chicken tikka
masala
p.100

lamb stew

SERVES 6

An all-time favourite, and brilliant every time. Rustic, simple and hearty.

1kg boned leg of lamb, trimmed and cut into 2cm pieces
Pinch of flaked sea salt
Grind of black pepper
2 tbsp plain flour
50g butter
1 tbsp olive oil
2 cloves of garlic, peeled and chopped
2 sprigs of rosemary
2 tbsp sunflower oil
1 large onion, halved and sliced
2 medium carrots, peeled and roughly chopped into 1cm dice
½ medium swede, peeled and roughly chopped into 1cm dice
1 litre vegetable or lamb stock
400g tinned chopped tomatoes
2 fresh bay leaves
2 tbsp roughly chopped flat leaf parsley

Preheat the oven to 160°c.

Season the lamb well with salt and pepper then dust it with the flour. In a large frying pan over a high heat, combine the butter, olive oil, garlic and rosemary. Once the butter has melted and is bubbling, place the floured lamb into the pan to sear. You may wish to do this in two batches, as you don't want to crowd the pan. Use tongs to keep turning each piece of meat until the lamb is browned and sealed on all sides. Keep the browned lamb, garlic and rosemary to one side.

Heat the sunflower oil in a large casserole dish, then add the onion, carrots and swede. Cook for 10 minutes until they are starting to caramelise. Add the stock, tomatoes and bay leaves. Simmer for 10 minutes, and then add the lamb, garlic and rosemary.

Cover the casserole dish with a lid and place it into the centre of the preheated oven. Cook the stew for 3 hours, stirring well after each hour. If the stew looks too wet at the end of the cooking time, just pop it back into the oven for an extra 30 minutes. If it's drying out at any point, add a little more water to bring it back to life. Remove the bay leaves and rosemary sprigs before serving.

Delicious served with potato mash (p.178) or fresh baguette. Top with chopped parsley to finish. Enjoy.

oxtail stew

SERVES 6

Oh my word. This is the stickiest, yummiest stew ever. I know the idea of using the tail of a cow may raise your eyebrows, but seriously, it makes the most incredibly rich and delicious stew. This tastes insanely good as well as filling the whole house with an amazing smell.

1kg oxtail
3 tbsp plain flour
Pinch of flaked sea salt
Grind of black pepper
3-4 tbsp sunflower oil
2 onions, halved and thinly sliced
2 cloves of garlic, peeled and sliced
2 carrots, peeled and cut into 2cm dice
2 sticks of celery, cut into 2cm dice
3 sprigs of thyme
2 fresh bay leaves
800ml beef stock
400ml good red wine
400g tinned chopped tomatoes
1 tbsp finely chopped flat leaf parsley

Preheat the oven to 160°c.

Coat the oxtail in the flour, tossing well to coat every piece, then season with salt and pepper.

Heat two tablespoons of the oil in a large frying pan. Using tongs, brown the oxtail over a medium heat for about 10 minutes, turning every now and then, until dark brown all over. You may need to add extra oil if the pan looks dry at any point during the browning step. Remove the oxtail and set aside.

Add more oil to the same pan, and fry the onions, garlic, carrots and celery for around 5 minutes until the vegetables start to caramelise.

Transfer the browned oxtail to a large casserole dish, followed by the vegetables, thyme and bay leaves. Cover everything with the stock, wine and tinned tomatoes. Season well with salt and pepper and give it a gentle but firm mix to ensure the liquid gets distributed throughout and under the oxtail. If the liquid does not quite cover the meat, add 100ml of water to ensure it's all submerged. This may be the case if your oxtail is from the fatter end of the tail.

Place the lid on the casserole dish and bring the stew to a gentle simmer on the stove. Transfer it to the oven and cook for 1 hour 30 minutes, take it out to give it a gentle stir, then put the stew back in for a further 1 hour and 30 minutes. The meat will start to fall off the bone and the sauce will be thick, glossy and sticky. If the stew looks too wet, just pop it back into the oven for an extra 30 minutes. If it's drying out at any point, then add a little more water to bring it back to life.

I like to serve this as it comes, with potato mash (p.178) or fresh baguette alongside. The oxtail bones and any gristly bits will simply fall away as you lift them out of the stew, and you can discard these. Top the stew with chopped parsley to finish. Enjoy.

carrot and coriander soup

SERVES 4

This is a constant go-to in my house. It's so comforting and so simple to make. On a cold evening, when there isn't much in the fridge, or you simply have little time, this will fill you, and everyone around you, up well.

1 tbsp sunflower oil
1 onion, chopped
1 clove of garlic, peeled and sliced
1 tsp ground coriander
450g carrots, peeled and roughly chopped
1 litre vegetable or chicken stock
Pinch of whole nutmeg, grated
2 tbsp chopped fresh coriander
Pinch of flaked sea salt
Grind of black pepper

Heat the oil in a large saucepan, add the onion and fry for 5 minutes until softened. Stir in the garlic and ground coriander, letting them cook for a couple of minutes.

Add your carrots and chosen stock. Bring to the boil, then reduce the heat to a simmer. Cover with a lid and cook for 20 minutes until the carrots are tender. Stir in the nutmeg.

Take the pan off the heat, and using an immersion blender, start to blitz up the soup. Throw in half of the fresh coriander halfway through, then continue to blend until smooth.

Taste and season with salt and black pepper. Top the soup with the remaining coriander to finish.

leek and potato soup

SERVES 4

This is such a perfect winter warmer. The combination of leek and potato always works beautifully. A classic which will never get old.

1 tbsp sunflower oil
1 onion, halved and sliced
2 medium potatoes, peeled and cubed
3 medium leeks, sliced
1 litre vegetable or chicken stock
Pinch of flaked sea salt
Grind of black pepper

Heat the oil in a large pan and add the onion, potatoes and leeks. Cook for 3 to 4 minutes until the vegetables are starting to soften.

Add the stock and bring to the boil. Season well and simmer for 10 minutes until the potatoes are just tender.

Take off the heat, and using an immersion blender, blitz up the soup until smooth.

Taste to check the seasoning, add salt and black pepper if needed, then serve. Enjoy.

chicken ramen

SERVES 4

This is also amazing with salmon, beef, duck breast or even just vegetables. The broth is full of flavour and after a long day this really hits the spot. It's such a cleansing broth and I make it at least once a week.

4 skinless chicken breasts
Pinch of flaked sea salt
Grind of black pepper
1 tbsp sunflower oil
1 tsp sesame oil
3 tsp garlic, peeled and grated
2 tsp fresh ginger, peeled and grated
3 tbsp soy sauce
1 tbsp maple syrup
1.2 litres vegetable or chicken stock
200g shiitake mushrooms, thinly sliced
4 packs of dried ramen noodles
100g pak choi, sliced in half lengthways
2 soft boiled eggs (p.197)
Handful of fresh coriander
Pinch of togarashi
1 lime, cut into wedges

Preheat the oven to 180°c and season the chicken generously with salt and pepper.

Add the sunflower oil to a frying pan on a medium heat, then lay the chicken breasts into the pan. Cook for 5 minutes until the chicken is golden brown. Turn the breasts over and cook for another 5 minutes until golden on both sides.

Transfer the chicken breasts to a baking tray and roast them in the preheated oven for 15 minutes, until cooked through. Remove the chicken from the oven, transfer to a plate and cover loosely with foil until ready to serve.

Next, make the ramen broth. Heat the sesame oil in a large pot over a medium heat, until simmering. Add the garlic and ginger, cook for a few minutes until softened, then add the soy sauce and maple syrup. Stir to combine then cook for another minute. Add the stock, cover the pan, and bring to the boil.

Remove the lid, turn the heat down, simmer the broth uncovered for 10 minutes, then add the mushrooms. Simmer gently for a further 10 minutes to allow all the flavours to develop.

Add extra salt to taste then add the ramen noodles and pak choi to the broth and cook for 2 to 3 minutes. Once they are ready, use tongs to divide the noodles and vegetables between bowls. Top with your sliced chicken breast (no end bits) and ladle over the broth.

Add half a soft boiled egg to each bowl along with some fresh coriander, togarashi and a lime wedge to serve.

chicken and prawn laksa

SERVES 4

Delicious, quick and easy: this makes everyone happy. You can make this vegan by using mushrooms and broccoli instead of chicken and prawns and omitting the fish sauce. The gentle hint of chilli and aromatic spices really warm you up. I always go back for seconds as it's just too good.

For the paste

3 cloves of garlic, peeled and roughly chopped

3cm fresh ginger or galangal, peeled and roughly chopped

2 shallots, peeled and roughly chopped

2 red bird's eye chillies

1 lemongrass stalk, chopped (white part only)

2 tbsp coriander stalks

50g palm sugar, grated

1 tbsp fish sauce

1 tsp each of ground turmeric, coriander and cumin

For the soup

2 tbsp coconut oil

400ml tinned coconut milk, shaken well before opening

500ml vegetable or chicken stock

500ml water

1 tbsp fish sauce

2 kaffir lime leaves

4 skinless chicken breasts

8 raw king prawns, peeled and deveined

300g flat rice noodles

Handful of coriander leaves

1 lime, cut into wedges

1 red bird's eye chilli (optional)

For the paste

Place all the ingredients for the paste into your food processor with two tablespoons of water, then blend until the paste forms.

For the soup

Heat the coconut oil in a large saucepan over a medium heat. Add your laksa paste and stir for 1 minute until fragrant, then add the coconut milk, stock and water. Bring to the boil. Add the fish sauce, lime leaves and whole chicken breasts. Poach the chicken in the broth for 10 minutes. Once cooked, using tongs, remove the chicken breasts and slice them thickly. Set the chicken aside on a plate and cover with foil to keep warm.

Add the prawns and noodles to the soup and then, once they are both cooked, use tongs to divide the noodles between bowls. Top with your sliced chicken breast (no end bits) and prawns, then ladle over the broth.

Serve with fresh coriander, place the lime wedges on the side for squeezing over the laksa and add extra chilli to taste.

Mains

pasta carbonara

This is a dish best eaten curled up on the sofa after a really long day. I rarely eat pasta or cream, but if I do, it's this dish. See (p.192) for a vegan carbonara sauce and vegan Parmesan recipe too.

150g streaky bacon, chopped
1 clove of garlic, peeled and grated
½ onion, finely diced
1 tbsp sunflower oil
100g chestnut mushrooms, thinly sliced
Pinch of flaked sea salt
Grind of black pepper
400g spaghetti
1 tsp olive oil
2 egg yolks
150ml single cream
50g Parmesan block, finely grated
1 sprig of parsley, leaves finely chopped

In a dry pan, cook the bacon until it starts to get crispy, then set aside. Using the same pan, fry the garlic and onion in a tablespoon of oil until they are soft and translucent. Set aside, then fry the mushrooms until well cooked through and season. Take the pan off the heat.

Cook the pasta in a large saucepan of boiling water for 6 to 10 minutes (depending on whether it's fresh or dry). Cook until al dente, take a piece out carefully with a fork to taste, then drain and place back in the saucepan with a drizzle of olive oil. Use tongs to move it around so it doesn't all stick together.

While the pasta is cooking, in a large bowl, combine the egg yolks, cream and Parmesan with some salt and pepper. Mix well then add the cooked pasta into the bowl of sauce, so it coats the pasta really well. Add the bacon, garlic, onions and mushrooms, using tongs to distribute everything well. Sprinkle the carbonara with more black pepper and fresh parsley to serve, adding extra Parmesan if you like.

two ways with beef fillet

SERVES 4

When we are having a treat, or it's a special occasion, then beef fillet is my go-to. We have it so rarely that it's appreciated a whole lot more. It's expensive, so most people are afraid to spend so much and then overcook it. Just follow the below method and you really won't go wrong. Both ways are utterly delicious.

1kg beef fillet, trimmed and tied with kitchen string
1 tbsp sunflower oil

Garlic and Horseradish
1 tbsp malt vinegar
1 tbsp maple syrup
1 tbsp horseradish (fresh or jarred)
2 cloves of garlic, peeled and grated
2 tbsp olive oil
Pinch of flaked sea salt
Grind of black pepper

In a small bowl, combine your vinegar, maple syrup, horseradish, garlic, olive oil, a pinch of salt and the black pepper. Mix well, then rub the marinade liberally all over the beef fillet. Leave for at least 10 minutes so the beef takes on the flavour, longer if you have time. Add more salt and pepper before cooking; the salt will give the beef a lovely crust.

Umami Goodness
6 tbsp fish sauce

Rub fish sauce over the fillet in the same way and marinate the beef; the longer the better. It's such a simple trick but tastes incredible.

To cook the fillet

Preheat the oven to 200°c.

Add the sunflower oil to a large frying pan over a high heat, and then carefully place the marinated fillet into it using tongs. Turn the fillet after it has had 2 minutes left untouched on each side, until browned and sealed well all over, including the ends. Transfer the fillet to a roasting tin and cook in the preheated oven for 10 minutes for rare, 15 minutes for medium rare or 20 minutes for medium.

Cover the beef with foil to keep it warm and leave to rest properly for 10 minutes before slicing, as thick or thinly as you like. You can head down various routes with a beautifully cooked fillet: a roast with all the trimmings, steak and chips, a noodle dish such as ramen, or serve with a simple salad or vegetables.

prawns with chilli, ginger & garlic butter

SERVES 4

Cooked on the barbecue or griddle, these are quick and easy to prepare,
and a wonderful way to enjoy prawns and get stuck in.

100g unsalted butter, chopped and softened
2 cloves of garlic, peeled and grated
1cm fresh ginger, peeled and grated
½ red bird's eye chilli, finely chopped
½ tsp flaked sea salt
1-2 tbsp fresh parsley, finely chopped
1 tbsp sunflower oil
16 large raw prawns, deveined with shells on
Grind of black pepper
1 lemon, cut into wedges

Place the butter, garlic, ginger, chilli and salt in a small saucepan over a medium heat until the butter has melted and is bubbling. Remove the pan from the heat and stir in a tablespoon of chopped parsley.

Heat a barbecue or griddle pan and using a silicone brush, brush the grill rack or pan with the sunflower oil.

Thread the prawns onto 16 metal skewers from the tail, so the heads are at the top of the skewer. Place each prawn skewer on the heat and cook for 3 minutes on each side, until they are pink and you can see some charring. Brush the prawns while cooking with your flavoured butter. If they are really large prawns, you can cook them for a little longer, but it's better to undercook fresh prawns, as the residual heat will finish the process, than to overcook them, making them hard and dry.

Place the cooked prawn skewers onto a platter, and pour over the remaining flavoured butter. Top with parsley, a pinch of salt and a grind of black pepper.

Serve with the lemon wedges. These are delicious peeled and dipped in aioli (p.190). Have a finger bowl and lots of kitchen paper available.

slow cooked lamb shoulder

SERVES 4

This is just heavenly, and fills the whole house with an amazing aroma. The finished dish is sweet, sticky,
delicious and so versatile too; you can enjoy the lamb with sweet potato mash (p.178)
and garlic green beans (p.175) from the Vegetables chapter, or as part of a Moroccan style spread (p.140).

1 large onion, halved and sliced
1 sprig of rosemary
4 cloves of garlic, skin on
2 tbsp olive oil
100ml malt vinegar
80g coconut sugar, plus extra to top
8 anchovy fillets, finely chopped
4 cloves of garlic, peeled and cut into slivers
4 sprigs of rosemary, leaves only
Pinch of flaked sea salt
Grind of black pepper
2kg lamb shoulder, bone in
400ml good white wine

Preheat the oven to 170°c.

Layer the sliced onion down the centre of a large roasting tin, add the rosemary and whole garlic cloves, then drizzle a tablespoon of olive oil over the top.

Place the vinegar, coconut sugar, remaining oil, anchovies, sliced garlic, rosemary leaves, salt and pepper into a bowl and stir to combine. Carefully make deep slits all over the lamb with a sharp knife, then pour the marinade over the meat, pushing the garlic slivers and rosemary leaves into the slits. Really get in there with your hands to massage the mixture in well and keep spooning the marinade over the meat so it seeps into the cuts.

Place the lamb on the bed of sliced onions, sprinkle with some extra coconut sugar and liberally season with salt and pepper. Pour the white wine around the lamb. Cover the roasting tin tightly with foil and roast the lamb for 3 hours in the preheated oven. For the last 10 minutes, remove the foil and allow the top to get some good colour and brown nicely.

Dish this up at the table, you just need two forks to break it apart and serve with the pan juices.

paella

SERVES 4

You don't need a specific paella pan for this, but it is nice to own one, especially if serving this al fresco; the joy on everyone's face when you carry it out is so wonderful. It's great for a weekend lunch and entertaining, as it's not too much work. This recipe is easily adaptable too; swap out the seafood and chicken for green beans, extra tomatoes and mushrooms to go veggie.

5 tbsp sunflower oil
4 chicken thighs, skinless and boneless
150g chorizo, cut into small dice
2 cloves of garlic, peeled and finely sliced
1 medium onion, finely diced
1 red bell pepper, finely diced
1½ litres vegetable or chicken stock
½ tsp saffron strands
350g paella rice
1 tsp smoked paprika
12 small clams, cleaned
12 mussels, cleaned and debearded
100g frozen peas
1 large tomato, cut into small dice
4 cloves of garlic, peeled and sliced
12 large raw prawns, deveined
1 medium squid, cleaned and sliced into rings
4 langoustines (optional)
5 tbsp chopped flat leaf parsley
Pinch of flaked sea salt
Grind of black pepper
1 lemon, cut into wedges

Add a tablespoon of sunflower oil to a frying pan over a medium heat. Fry the chicken thighs and leave them to brown for 3 minutes on each side, put to one side, and cover with foil to keep warm.

Next, heat two tablespoons of oil in a paella or large frying pan over a medium heat. Add the chorizo and fry until the oils are starting to release, then add the garlic, onion and pepper to cook until softened. Meanwhile, heat the chicken stock in a saucepan and add the saffron into it. Mix well. Now add the paella rice to the paella pan and stir quickly until all the grains are completely coated and glossy. Add the paprika and pour in the hot saffron chicken stock. Wedge the chicken thighs deeply in the rice with just the tops showing.

Over the next 15 minutes, add extra water, 100ml at a time, as the rice starts to absorb the stock. Be careful not to add too much though, and stay with it, as you don't want the bottom layer to catch and burn or the rice to dry out. Add the clams, mussels, peas and chopped tomato, then continue to cook the gently bubbling paella for another 10 to 15 minutes while it continues to absorb liquid.

Clean and dry your chicken pan, heat one tablespoon of oil and then add half the garlic. Once it has started to brown, add the prawns two or three at a time so you don't overcrowd the pan. Cook on both sides until all the prawns are done, adding a little more oil if needed. Place on a plate lined with kitchen paper to absorb excess grease, then add the prawns to your paella.

Clean and dry the pan again, place on a medium heat and add the last tablespoon of oil. When the oil is really bubbling, add the remaining garlic and then the squid rings. Give them 10 seconds in the pan to get some colour, turning to cook both sides, then evenly distribute the squid in the paella. Finally, add the langoustines (if using) to the frying pan and allow the heat to cook them on all sides for 1 minute. Carefully transfer them into the paella.

Scatter the chopped parsley over the paella, season with salt and pepper then serve immediately with lots of lemon wedges and aioli (p.190).

two ways with roast chicken

Roast chicken and all the trimmings is a very important winter Sunday lunch tradition in our household, and it is my absolute favourite thing. It makes me so happy; it's pure joy to have family time over a roast, followed by sticky toffee pudding (p.241) and then board games or a mid-afternoon nap.

1 whole chicken (approx. 1½kg)
Pinch of flaked sea salt
Grind of black pepper

Preheat the oven to 180°c.

Lemon and Thyme
1 lemon, halved
2 sprigs of thyme
50g butter, softened

Season the cavity of the chicken liberally with salt and pepper, then stuff it with both lemon halves and the thyme. Rub the butter over the skin, covering it completely, and season well.

Garlic Butter
100g butter, softened
3 cloves of garlic, peeled and grated
1 sprig of fresh parsley leaves, finely chopped

In a bowl, mix three quarters of the butter with the grated garlic, chopped parsley, a good pinch of salt and a grind of pepper. With your fingers, work slowly and carefully to loosen the chicken skin and push the flavoured butter underneath. Take care not to tear the skin. Reach all the way across each of the breasts to get the garlic butter distributed evenly. Rub all the remaining butter over the skin and then sprinkle with salt quite liberally to help it crisp up well.

To cook the chicken

Place the prepared chicken into a roasting tin and cook in the centre of your preheated oven for 1 hour and 30 minutes. As it starts to get brown and crispy, spoon the juices or melted garlic butter back over the chicken. Check that the chicken is cooked by making a slit in the thigh with a sharp knife. If there is any trace of blood or the flesh still seems pink, put the chicken back into the oven. Remember that if you have used a larger chicken than specified here, it will need a longer cooking time. Once the juices run clear, you are all set. Lift your chicken onto a chopping board with two large forks then leave to rest for 5 minutes.

If you are making a roast, this works best with the lemon and thyme chicken, and you could serve it with roast potatoes (p.181) and honey roasted carrots (p.172) from the Vegetables chapter with greens and gravy (p.193). If you opt for a simple rustic lunch or dinner, any of the dishes from the Salads chapters would be a great match.

I like to divide the chicken up with 'cut me' lines where all the joins are, so that everyone gets a little breast, leg and wing. Make sure you turn the chicken over to dig out the delicious oysters too. Present on a platter with all your accompaniments of choice. If there's any left, use the meat in sandwich or wrap fillings, and the carcass is always a great base for a good stock.

three ways with salmon

I regularly buy a whole salmon, scaled and filleted. I then pin bone and portion it up to freeze, so that I always have some in the house. I often used to make the pesto and Parmesan salmon for guests on super yachts for a delicious lunch. The Asian versions are spicy and if like me, you adore a chilli kick, you will love them.

thai salmon

SERVES 4

Delicious with coconut rice, fresh mango slices, coriander and lime wedges.

1 green bird's eye chilli, roughly chopped
1 clove of garlic, peeled and chopped
1cm fresh ginger or galangal, peeled and roughly chopped
3 kaffir lime leaves, roughly chopped and stems removed
2 lemongrass stalks, roughly chopped (white part only)
1 tbsp coconut oil
1 tbsp soy sauce
2 tbsp fish sauce
50g palm sugar, grated
2 tbsp lime juice
4 200g skinless salmon fillets, pin boned

Preheat the grill to 200°c.

Place the chilli, garlic, ginger or galangal, lime leaves and lemongrass into a food processor and blitz really well until all the fibres have broken down into a paste. Heat the coconut oil in a small saucepan then add the paste, stirring it around for 1 minute to cook before adding the soy sauce, fish sauce and palm sugar. Mix well and cook for 1 minute until the sugar has dissolved, then add the lime juice and remove the pan from the heat.

Ensure there are no remaining bones in the salmon and place the upside down fillets on a baking tray lined with foil. Cook under the preheated grill for 5 minutes, remove from the oven and, very carefully with a small angled palette knife and your fingers, gently turn each piece of salmon over, being very careful not to break the fillets. Add the paste gently but liberally to the top, forming a crust, and place back under the grill until bubbling and browning.

chilli glazed salmon skewers

SERVES 4

These are my absolute favourite, served with coconut rice and Thai green salad (p.160).

2 tbsp Thai chilli jam (p.195)
400ml tinned coconut milk, shaken well before opening
1 tsp tamarind paste
1 tbsp lime juice
1 tbsp fish sauce
1 kaffir lime leaf, thinly sliced
4 200g skinless salmon fillets, pin boned and cut into 3cm cubes
1 tbsp sunflower oil

In a small saucepan over a medium heat, bring the chilli jam and coconut milk to a simmer. Add the tamarind, lime juice, fish sauce and kaffir lime leaf then simmer for a few more minutes to reduce.

Preheat a griddle pan or barbecue to a medium heat. Thread the salmon cubes onto eight metal skewers, and brush both sides with the glaze.

Brush the grill rack or pan with the sunflower oil and cook the salmon, turning regularly, for 3 to 4 minutes or until charred. Brush with more glaze once cooked.

pesto and parmesan salmon

SERVES 4

Serve with oven roasted vine tomatoes or a big Mediterranean salad.

100g Parmesan block, in chunks
100g bread, broken into pieces
100g pesto (p.192)
1 tbsp olive oil
Pinch of flaked sea salt
Grind of black pepper
4 200g skinless salmon fillets, pin boned
1 lemon, zested

Place the Parmesan into the food processor first, whizz into breadcrumb-sized pieces, then pour into a bowl. Add the bread to the processor and whizz into actual breadcrumbs, then add the Parmesan back in along with the pesto, olive oil, a pinch of salt and a grind of black pepper. Blend until a wonderful bright green paste forms.

Ensure there are no remaining bones in the salmon and place on a baking tray lined with foil. Cook under the preheated grill for 5 minutes, remove from the oven and, very carefully with a small angled palette knife and your fingers, gently turn each piece of salmon over, being very careful not to break the fillets.

Liberally and evenly spread your breadcrumb mixture over the top of the salmon, pushing it down so the crust sticks to the fish. Finish by sprinkling more mixture over the top without pressing it down, so that when the crust cooks it will have great texture. Place back under the grill until brown.

Top the cooked salmon with lemon zest. Enjoy.

pizza

SERVES 6

Making pizza at home is very simple and once you've tried it, you'll do it time and time again. It's great to make with my boys, letting them get hands-on and choosing our own toppings.

For the bases

14g dried yeast

1 tbsp honey or maple syrup

2 tbsp olive oil, plus extra for greasing the foil

650ml lukewarm water

800g tipo 00 flour, plus extra for dusting

200g semolina flour, plus extra for dusting

2 tsp Himalayan salt

For the sauce

400g tinned chopped tomatoes

1 clove of garlic, peeled and sliced

1 tbsp tomato purée

1 tbsp olive oil

1 tsp dried oregano

Pinch of flaked sea salt

Grind of black pepper

For the toppings

150g mozzarella

Chorizo or Serrano ham

Mushrooms

Red bell peppers

Anchovy fillets

Dried chilli flakes

Rocket

Basil

For the bases

In a small bowl, add the yeast, honey or maple syrup and olive oil to the lukewarm water. Mix everything together and leave for 10 minutes until the yeast starts to activate, bubble and come to life. If the water is too cold it won't activate the yeast, if it's too hot, it will kill it.

In a large bowl, combine the flours and salt. Make a well in the centre then pour in the liquid, gradually mixing in the flours with a wooden spoon until a mass of dough begins to form.

Turn the dough out and knead on a lightly floured work surface for about 10 minutes until soft and smooth. You can of course use a electric stand mixer and dough hook instead, which saves a lot of time.

Transfer the dough to a lightly oiled bowl, cover with cling film and leave in a warm place to prove for 1 hour or until it's doubled in size.

Punch down the proven dough well, transfer to a lightly floured surface and divide the dough into six individual balls. Working with one ball at a time, and using a lightly floured rolling pin, roll the dough out into your preferred pizza size. Tear off sheets of foil just bigger than each pizza. Grease the foil all over with some olive oil and liberally sprinkle with semolina flour, then place the pizza base on top. Repeat with each ball of dough.

For the sauce

Place the tinned tomatoes into a food processor with the garlic, purée and olive oil. Blitz until smooth then transfer to a small saucepan over a medium heat and cook for 5 minutes. Stir through the oregano and season the sauce to taste with salt and pepper. Add the sauce to your pizza bases, spreading it out from the centre but leaving the edge clear to create a crust.

To assemble and cook your pizza

Remove all the racks and preheat the oven to its highest temperature, usually around 240°c.

Add your mozzarella, and any other toppings you wish. Carefully slide the pizza with foil base onto the base of the oven. Cook for 8 to 10 minutes, until the pizzas are golden brown and the cheese is fully melted. Add any cold toppings, such as Serrano ham, fresh basil or rocket, after cooking. Repeat this process to cook each pizza then serve.

roasted
mediterranean veg
p.180

pomegranate
dressing
p.189

slow cooked
lamb shoulder
p.128

HENRYWOOD

tomato and
pomegranate salad
p.148

flatbreads and
plain hummus
p.72

three ways with chicken wings

Great in the oven or on the barbecue, these chicken wings are delicious all on their own or with coleslaw, corn on the cob and sweet potato wedges. These three delicious marinades work well for any meat, and the BBQ sauce makes a wonderful dip too.

16 chicken wings

Ginger and Honey Marinade

1 small red bird's eye chilli, finely chopped
1 clove of garlic, peeled and grated
2cm fresh ginger, peeled and grated
4 tbsp runny honey
3 tbsp soy sauce
1 tsp sesame oil
Pinch of flaked sea salt
Grind of black pepper

Mix all the ingredients together in a shallow bowl then rub the marinade into the chicken wings to coat them well. Leave for a minimum of 1 hour to marinate; the longer the better, so leave them in the fridge overnight if you are well prepared.

BBQ Sauce

55g coconut sugar
50ml soy sauce
300ml tomato ketchup (p.190)
Pinch of flaked sea salt
Grind of black pepper

Put the coconut sugar, soy sauce and tomato ketchup into a small saucepan over a medium heat and season with salt and pepper. Simmer for a few minutes to combine the flavours and ensure the sugar has dissolved.

Spice Rub

1 tsp Himalayan salt
1 tsp ground coriander
1 tbsp onion powder
1 tsp garlic powder
1 tsp smoked paprika
1 tsp ground cumin
½ tsp cayenne pepper
Grind of black pepper
¼ tsp dried chilli flakes
¼ tsp dried parsley
2 tbsp coconut sugar

This recipe makes 100g which is enough to use as one serving for any meat or fish. Pound all the ingredients together using a pestle and mortar until you have a powdery consistency.

To cook the wings

Preheat the oven to 180°c.

Place your marinated wings on a baking tray.

Place the prepared chicken wings into the centre of the oven to cook for 30 to 35 minutes until browned and sticky or crispy, depending on the flavouring.

If they are large wings, they may still look pale, so just put them back in until they get darker. Once you think the wings are done, make a slit with a sharp knife to check that the juices run clear, so you know they are ready to serve.

whole baked sea bass

SERVES 4

Every time I make this, we all devour it and say the very same thing: why don't we eat this more often? Don't be scared of filleting it on the table, because in fact it's so much easier to do when cooked this way, and I've outlined the steps below. This is a wonderful dish to enjoy with garlic green beans (p.175).

2 onions, halved and sliced
3 tbsp olive oil
2 cloves of garlic, peeled and sliced
1kg whole sea bass, gutted and scaled, or two smaller 500g ones
Pinch of flaked sea salt
Grind of black pepper
½ lemon, thinly sliced
1 fresh bay leaf
1 sprig of thyme
1 sprig of rosemary
100ml good white wine
½ lemon, cut into wedges

Preheat the oven to 200°c.

Layer the sliced onion down the centre of a large roasting tin, then drizzle a tablespoon of olive oil over the top. In a small bowl, mix the sliced garlic with the remaining olive oil.

Massage the fish gently with the garlic oil then place it on top of the onion layer; this way it won't stick to the bottom of the tin.

Season the cavity of the sea bass with salt and pepper then stuff a lemon slice inside with the bay leaf, thyme and rosemary.

Season the top of the fish liberally, then tie a few lemon slices in place on top with some kitchen string. Pour the white wine around the fish into the tin.

Place into the preheated oven and roast for 30 minutes. If you are using smaller fish, you can roast them for half the time. Transfer the fish to a chopping board and any pan juices into a small bowl. Discard the onions.

I like to serve this at the table and dish it all up there. Working from the head to the tail, gently cut along the backbone with a spoon to separate the flesh from the bone. Remove the backbone, fins and bones along the belly. Gently separate the head and tail.

Carefully lift off the top fillet and transfer it to a plate. Remove the head and spine by simply lifting them out and discarding the bones. Gently lift the second fillet onto the same plate. Drizzle with the pan juices before serving with the lemon wedges.

Salads

tomato and pomegranate salad

SERVES 4

This is a fresh and fruity salad, wonderful on its own as well as with a main. I love it served with a Moroccan spread like slow cooked lamb, couscous, hummus and flatbreads or even garlic roast chicken and quinoa.

For the salad
200g red cherry tomatoes, halved
200g yellow cherry tomatoes, halved
200g vine tomatoes, chopped into 1cm dice
1 red bell pepper, chopped into 1cm dice
1 yellow bell pepper, chopped into 1cm dice
1 small red onion, finely diced
1 medium pomegranate, deseeded
Handful of fresh coriander leaves
Pinch of flaked sea salt
Grind of black pepper

For the pomegranate dressing
See recipe on page 189

Add all the prepared tomatoes, peppers, onion and pomegranate seeds to a platter. Toss to distribute everything evenly. Drizzle the pomegranate dressing over the whole salad with a spoon and toss to coat everything well. Add the fresh coriander, and season well with salt and pepper before serving.

lentils with maple and cumin roasted carrots

SERVES 4

Such a simple dish but really tasty and filling. It works well with roast chicken or slow cooked lamb,
or just with a vegetable selection and hummus.

For the salad

300g carrots, peeled and quartered
lengthways, or baby carrots kept whole
2 tsp cumin seeds
2 tbsp olive oil
3 tbsp maple syrup
1 tbsp sunflower oil
2 cloves of garlic, peeled and sliced
1 small red onion, thinly sliced
400g tinned brown lentils, drained and
rinsed
20g fresh coriander leaves, chopped
20g fresh mint leaves, chopped

For the garlic and caper dressing

1 clove of garlic, peeled and grated
1 lemon, zested and juiced
2 tsp capers, drained
2 tbsp olive oil
Pinch of flaked sea salt
Grind of black pepper

For the salad

Preheat the oven to 200°c.

Add the carrots and cumin seeds to a large roasting tin and drizzle over the olive oil. Roast in the preheated oven for 20 minutes until cooked and starting to caramelise. Brush each piece of carrot well with the maple syrup then cook for a further 5 minutes.

Meanwhile, heat the sunflower oil in a frying pan then add the garlic and red onion and cook for a few minutes until softened. Add the lentils. Leave on the heat while stirring for a couple of minutes, and then pour the lentil mixture into a large serving bowl or platter.

For the garlic and caper dressing

Stir the ingredients for the dressing together in a small bowl.

Add the roasted carrots, coriander and mint to the lentils and toss together. Season well, then drizzle the dressing liberally all over the warm salad. Finish with extra herbs and more black pepper.

coleslaw

SERVES 4

This is my favourite accompaniment, especially in summer with barbecued chicken wings, corn on the cob and couscous. You can use the vegan mayonnaise (p.190), and I also love using the maple and tahini dressing (p.188) with the addition of grated celeriac and dried cranberries.

¼ red cabbage
¼ white cabbage
1 small red onion
2 carrots
4 tbsp mayonnaise
1 tbsp Dijon mustard
1 tbsp lemon juice
Pinch of flaked sea salt
Grind of black pepper
Fresh parsley leaves, chopped

First, prepare your vegetables. Remove the hard core from the cabbages, then finely slice the leaves. Peel, halve and finely slice the onion. Peel and grate the carrots. Alternatively, if you have a slicing attachment on your food processor, use that instead because it saves lots of time and makes the vegetables really fine.

Mix the red and white cabbage, onion and carrot in a large bowl. Add the mayonnaise and mix well, then stir in the Dijon mustard, lemon juice, salt, pepper and most of the parsley. Mix until everything has been well incorporated. I like to do this with my hands so I know it's all properly coated.

Serve the coleslaw topped with the remaining fresh parsley and more freshly ground black pepper.

greek salad

SERVES 4

My go-to salad when I am short on time. It is very versatile and can be served with my oven baked sea bass or a roast chicken and maple roasted sweet potatoes among other things.

100g mixed leaves
100g Kalamata olives
100g cherry tomatoes, halved
100g feta, cut into 1cm cubes
1 small red onion, finely sliced
½ cucumber, halved and sliced
½ red bell pepper, sliced
Fresh basil leaves
2 tbsp olive oil
2 tbsp balsamic vinegar
Pinch of flaked sea salt
Grind of black pepper

Add the mixed leaves, olives, tomatoes, feta, red onion, cucumber, red pepper and basil to a large bowl and mix together to combine well. Drizzle the oil and balsamic over the top and season with salt and pepper to taste. Serve and enjoy.

prawn caesar salad

It took me a long time to love Caesar salad because often it just isn't done properly, but this balance of ingredients works so well. You can make this salad on its own, as a side, or with chicken instead, which I've included instructions for below.

1 tbsp sunflower oil

12 king prawns, peeled and deveined (leave the tails on) or 4 chicken breasts

2 slices of bread, cut into 2cm rustic cubes

1 tbsp olive oil

Pinch of flaked sea salt

Grind of black pepper

4 gem lettuces

20g Parmesan block

For the Caesar dressing
See recipe on page 189

Preheat the oven to 180°c.

Put the sunflower oil in a frying pan over a medium heat then add the prawns. Allow them to cook for 3 minutes, then turn over and cook for a further 3 minutes on the other side until fully pink and cooked through. Remove and set aside.

In a bowl, drizzle your cubed bread with the olive oil and mix with your hands. Scatter the cubes of bread onto a baking tray and place in the preheated oven for 10 minutes, until the cubes are golden.

If you prefer your Caesar salad with chicken, season the breasts generously with salt and pepper. Add the sunflower oil to a frying pan on a medium heat then lay the chicken breasts into the pan and cook for 5 minutes until golden brown. Turn over and cook for another 5 minutes, until golden all over.

Transfer the chicken breasts to a baking tray, and place into the preheated oven. Roast for 15 minutes, until the chicken is cooked through.

Cut the bottom stem off the gem lettuces then wash and separate the leaves. You can roughly chop them or leave them whole as preferred. Pour the Caesar dressing over the leaves and mix together using two spoons to coat them all well.

Place the prawns onto your salad, or slice up your cooked chicken breasts, and top with a handful of your baked croutons and liberal shavings of Parmesan. Use a potato peeler for this to get lovely thin curls. Enjoy.

feta, cranberry and pistachio couscous

I have been making this recipe forever. I always thought couscous was bland and boring, but once I made this using pretty much what I had to hand at the time, it stuck. This is a great addition to a barbecue or lunch spread. Everyone always comments on it. You'll find it a really easy go-to, as it's a gorgeous accompaniment to most dishes.

200g couscous
300ml boiling water
4 tbsp olive oil
1 lemon, juiced
Pinch of flaked sea salt
100g pistachios
100g dried cranberries
100g feta cheese, cut into 1cm cubes
10g fresh parsley leaves, roughly chopped
10g fresh coriander leaves, roughly chopped
10g fresh basil leaves, roughly chopped
10g fresh mint leaves, roughly chopped
Grind of black pepper

Place the couscous in a clear heatproof bowl, pour over the boiling water, cover the bowl with cling film and leave the couscous to stand for 5 minutes or until all the water has been absorbed.

Fluff it all up with a fork, adding a touch more water if it seems dry. Stir in the olive oil, lemon juice and salt and mix well. Pop your pistachios into the food processor, and allow them go somewhere beyond chopped to a textured dust, as this adds a really lovely green colour to the couscous.

Fold the crushed pistachios and dried cranberries through the couscous to distribute them evenly. Then stir through the cubes of feta, gently so they don't break. Add all your chopped herb leaves.

Before serving the couscous, add more olive oil and lemon juice to taste, or if the mix seems dry. This is especially important the next day once it's been in the fridge. Season it with extra salt and black pepper too, if needed. Enjoy.

spicy green papaya salad

This is one of my favourite salads: amazing on its own, or as part of a Thai style spread (p.86). If you can't get your hands on a green papaya, just use a normal one, or even a firm mango works well too. You can omit the fish sauce and shrimps to make this a vegan salad.

4 tbsp dried baby shrimps
50g peanuts
2 cloves of garlic, peeled and roughly chopped
2cm fresh ginger, peeled and roughly chopped
1 lime, juiced
1 red bird's eye chilli, roughly chopped
3 tbsp palm sugar, grated
2 tbsp soy sauce
4 tbsp fish sauce
2 tbsp tamarind paste
15 green beans, trimmed
10 cherry tomatoes, halved
1 medium green papaya, peeled and deseeded then finely sliced
Handful of fresh mint, roughly chopped
Handful of fresh Thai basil, roughly chopped
Handful of fresh coriander, roughly chopped
1 lime, quartered

Soak the dried baby shrimps in boiling water for 10 minutes, then drain them. Meanwhile, toast the peanuts in a dry pan over a medium heat until golden brown, then set aside to cool.

Place the soaked shrimps and half the toasted peanuts in a food processor along with the garlic, ginger, lime juice, chilli, palm sugar, soy sauce, fish sauce and tamarind paste. Blitz until everything has blended into a loose paste.

Place the green beans, tomatoes and papaya into a large bowl. Mix the paste through the salad until it coats the beans, tomatoes and papaya well. Mix the herbs through the salad.

Scatter the remaining toasted peanuts over the top, and squeeze over some extra lime juice to taste before serving.

thai green salad

SERVES 4

This is a great big green raw salad. It takes a little work, but is absolutely delicious. Utterly perfect with salmon and prawns, or just on its own. You can use any combination of greens you like, as long as everything is completely fresh. You must not skip the garlic and shallots though; these and the tamarind dressing bring the salad alive and you won't want to stop eating it.

For the garnish

300ml sunflower oil

5 cloves of garlic, peeled and finely sliced

3 shallots, peeled and finely sliced

50g white sesame seeds

For the salad

1 cucumber, peeled into ribbons

100g asparagus, peeled into ribbons

100g pak choi, finely sliced

100g green beans, trimmed

50g tenderstem broccoli, sliced

50g kohlrabi, finely sliced

50g fresh dill, pulled apart (keep the length)

50g fresh coriander leaves, roughly chopped

50g fresh mint leaves, roughly chopped

50g fresh Thai basil leaves, roughly chopped

For the tamarind dressing

See recipe on page 189

For the garnish

Pour approximately 3cm of sunflower oil into a large deep frying pan and place on a medium heat.

Using a slotted spoon, lower the garlic and shallots into the hot oil in batches. They won't take long to crisp up and go brown. Be careful as they can turn from golden to black and burnt very fast.

Transfer the crispy garlic and shallot garnish to a plate lined with plenty of kitchen paper to absorb excess oil. Repeat the process until it is all done, working in batches to avoid lowering the oil temperature.

In a dry pan, toast the sesame seeds. Keep a close eye on the pan so they don't burn. Pour the toasted seeds into a spice grinder and blitz to a powder.

For the salad

Combine all the green vegetables and herbs in a large serving bowl. Add the tamarind dressing, a liberal dose of the toasted sesame powder, and the fried shallots and garlic. Mix everything together well and serve immediately.

fig, mozzarella and serrano salad

SERVES 4

This is such a beautiful salad. You can swap the fresh figs with ripe peaches or nectarines if you like. It's just perfect all on its own for a lunch, or as part of a bigger spread.

100g mixed leaves
4 ripe figs, halved
2 large balls of buffalo mozzarella
8 slices of quality Serrano ham
Handful of fresh basil leaves

For the honey and lemon dressing
See recipe on page 188

Place the mixed leaves onto your platter and add the freshly cut figs with the inside facing upwards so everyone can see the beautiful fruit inside. Tear bite-size pieces from the mozzarella balls and scatter them around the salad, then twist your Serrano ham slices and lay them between the figs and cheese so there is a visually even spread. Distribute the basil leaves over the top.

Drizzle the dressing liberally all over the salad with a spoon, especially over the figs (if they are not quite in season, the honey will sweeten them nicely). Season the dressed salad with more salt and another grind of black pepper, then serve immediately with fresh bread on the side.

butternut squash, feta and chorizo salad

SERVES 4

There is something very satisfying about this salad in winter time. I love to pair it with a roast chicken and tear that up into it too for an even more satisfying winter meal.

1kg butternut squash
2 tbsp olive oil
Pinch of flaked sea salt
Grind of black pepper
½ chorizo, thinly sliced
2 handfuls of rocket
2 handfuls of baby spinach
200g feta cheese
6 tbsp olive oil
4 tbsp balsamic vinegar

Preheat the oven to 200°c.

Peel and deseed the butternut squash, then cut the flesh into 2cm cubes. Place the butternut squash into a roasting tin, drizzle the olive oil all over then season with salt and pepper. I like to get in there with my hands and ensure the oil is thoroughly coating the cubes. Roast for 30 minutes in the preheated oven, giving the tin a shake around half way through. Remove once the squash is turning brown and caramelised, then set aside to cool.

While the butternut squash is roasting, place the chorizo slices into a large frying pan over a medium heat in a single layer. Once they start curling at the edges, turn them over with tongs to cook the other side for just a minute. Transfer the chorizo onto a plate lined with kitchen paper to absorb the excess oil, then leave to cool. Discard the oil in the pan.

In a large bowl or serving platter, mix the rocket and spinach leaves together. Crumble over your feta and add the roasted butternut squash and chorizo. Then add your oil and balsamic, toss the salad well with serving spoons, season to taste with salt and pepper, and serve.

mediterranean quinoa salad

SERVES 6

Simple and delicious on its own as a satisfying lunch bowl, or as an accompaniment to most dishes.

For the salad

400g butternut squash, peeled, deseeded and chopped into 2cm cubes

1 tbsp olive oil

Pinch of flaked sea salt

Grind of black pepper

300g quinoa, rinsed

100g Kalamata black olives, pitted and sliced

100g sun-dried tomatoes, finely sliced

100g dried cranberries

40g flaked almonds, toasted

20g fresh basil, roughly chopped

20g fresh parsley, roughly chopped

For the Mediterranean dressing

3 tbsp lemon juice

3 tbsp olive oil

3 tbsp balsamic vinegar

For the salad

Preheat the oven to 200°c.

Place the butternut squash into a roasting tin, drizzle the olive oil all over then season with salt and pepper. I like to get in there with my hands and ensure the oil is thoroughly coating the cubes. Roast for 30 minutes in the preheated oven, giving the tin a shake around half way through.

While the butternut squash is roasting, cook the quinoa. Place it in a pan with 500ml of water, bring it to the boil and then reduce the heat to let it simmer for 12 to 14 minutes. Drain once cooked, then spread the quinoa out on a large tray to cool.

For the Mediterranean dressing

Put all the ingredients into a jar or bowl and shake or whisk well until thoroughly combined.

Add the olives, sun-dried tomatoes, cranberries and flaked almonds (reserving some for garnish) to the quinoa. Mix well then gently fold through the roasted butternut squash without crushing the cubes. Add the herbs, keeping back a few leaves for garnish, then season the salad with salt and pepper. Pour the dressing over and top with the reserved almonds and herbs to finish.

Vegetables

Vegetables are such an important part of everyday eating. This chapter is full of many of my favourite ways to enjoy vegetables, which you can match up with dishes from my other savoury chapters to really enhance your lunch or dinner feasting.

honey roasted carrots

SERVES 4

500g carrots, peeled and trimmed
(approx. 3 large carrots)
3 tbsp runny honey or maple syrup
1 tbsp lemon juice
2 sprigs of thyme
2 tbsp olive oil
Pinch of flaked sea salt
Grind of black pepper

Preheat your oven to 200°c.

Chop the carrots lengthways into quarters, to form batons. In a bowl, mix the honey or maple syrup with the lemon juice and thyme leaves.

Place the carrots on a large baking tray, drizzle them with the oil, brush them with the honey glaze and then season well with salt and pepper.

Roast the carrots in the preheated oven for 15 minutes, then brush them again with the honey and lemon mixture. Give them a good stir to coat each baton thoroughly.

Place the tray back in the oven for a further 5 minutes, then repeat the glazing step one more time. After three glazes and a final 5 minutes, the carrots will be softened, glossy and delicious.

Season with salt and pepper before serving.

asparagus and parmesan

SERVES 4

800g asparagus
50g Parmesan block
½ lemon
1 tbsp olive oil
Pinch of flaked sea salt
Grind of black pepper

Remove the woody ends of the asparagus by trimming 2½cm off the bottom of each spear, ensuring they all look similar in length.

Cook the asparagus in a large saucepan of salted boiling water for 2 to 3 minutes until just tender, then drain.

Using a potato peeler, liberally shave the Parmesan all over the asparagus. Dress with a good squeeze of lemon juice and a drizzle of olive oil.

Season with sea salt and black pepper to taste, then serve.

roasted turmeric cauliflower

SERVES 4

1 large head of cauliflower
2 cloves of garlic, peeled and sliced
2 tbsp olive oil
1 tsp ground cumin
1 tsp paprika
1 tsp ground turmeric
1 tsp ground ginger
Pinch of flaked sea salt
Grind of black pepper
Handful of fresh coriander, chopped

Preheat your oven to 220°c.

Chop the cauliflower into florets. Mix the cauliflower and garlic with the olive oil, cumin, paprika, turmeric, ginger, salt and black pepper. I suggest using gloves, so as not to stain your hands with the turmeric.

Place the spiced cauliflower in a single layer on a large baking tray. Roast for 10 minutes in the preheated oven or until the cauliflower is tender and charring.

Sprinkle with the fresh chopped coriander and serve.

roasted cherry tomatoes

SERVES 4

300g cherry tomatoes
2 tbsp olive oil
Pinch of flaked sea salt
Grind of black pepper

Preheat oven to 200°c.

Place the cherry tomatoes in a roasting tin, drizzle them with the olive oil and sprinkle with salt and pepper. Put them in the preheated oven for 6 minutes, until their skins are beginning to burst, then serve.

garlic green beans

SERVES 4

400g green beans, trimmed
2 cloves of garlic, peeled and grated
2 tbsp butter or olive oil
1 tbsp lemon juice
Pinch of flaked sea salt
Grind of black pepper

Cook the green beans in boiling salted water until tender, then drain and blanch them quickly in iced water. Drain and set aside.

In a frying pan over a medium heat, cook the garlic in butter or oil for 1 minute, then stir through the green beans until they are coated well. Add the lemon juice and season generously with salt and pepper to taste before serving.

roasted balsamic beetroot

SERVES 4

800g beetroot (approx. 3 or 4), scrubbed
and trimmed
100ml vegetable stock
1 tbsp balsamic vinegar
2 tbsp olive oil
2 sprigs of fresh thyme
2 tbsp runny honey or maple syrup
Pinch of flaked sea salt
Grind of black pepper

Preheat your oven to 200°c.

Cut each beetroot into four to six wedges and set aside.

Mix the stock, balsamic vinegar, oil, thyme leaves and honey or maple syrup in a bowl then add the beetroot wedges. Toss to ensure they are all well coated in the glaze. Season with salt and pepper.

Roast for 45 minutes in the preheated oven until the glaze is sticky and the beetroot is tender.

potato mash

SERVES 4

6 sweet or white potatoes,
peeled and chopped
110g butter, chopped into small pieces
2 cloves of garlic, peeled and grated
Pinch of flaked sea salt
Grind of black pepper

Place the potatoes into a large saucepan with enough salted water to cover them. Bring to the boil. Reduce the heat to medium-low and simmer for about 20 minutes until the potatoes are tender.

Tip the potatoes into a colander to drain them. Put the butter and garlic into the pan and heat until the butter is melted and the garlic starts to cook. Remove the pan from the heat and put the potatoes back in. With a potato masher, mash the potatoes with the butter, garlic, salt and pepper until smooth.

roasted broccoli, garlic, chilli & parmesan

SERVES 4

1 medium head of broccoli
4 tbsp olive oil
1 red bird's eye chilli, finely sliced
4 cloves of garlic, peeled and grated
Pinch of flaked sea salt
Grind of black pepper
40g Parmesan block

Preheat your oven to 220°c.

Chop the broccoli into florets and place them in a bowl. Toss the florets with the olive oil, chilli and garlic then season well with salt and black pepper.

Spread the broccoli out in a single layer on a large baking tray. Roast for 10 minutes in the preheated oven, or until the broccoli is tender and charring.

Using a potato peeler, liberally shave the Parmesan all over the broccoli. Serve immediately.

roasted mediterranean veg

SERVES 4

1 medium aubergine
1 medium courgette
1 medium red bell pepper, deseeded
1 red onion, quartered
2 sprigs of fresh thyme
2 sprigs of fresh rosemary
4 cloves of garlic, skins on
4 tbsp olive oil
1 tbsp balsamic vinegar
Pinch of flaked sea salt
Grind of black pepper
100g cherry tomatoes

Preheat the oven to 220°c.

Chop the aubergine, courgette and pepper into 2cm slices. All the pieces should be a similar size.

Spread the prepared vegetables along with the red onion evenly on a roasting tray with the thyme and rosemary leaves, and garlic. Drizzle with the olive oil and balsamic vinegar then season well with salt and pepper.

Roast the vegetables for 20 minutes in the preheated oven, remove from the oven and move them around, then add the cherry tomatoes. Cook for a further 10 minutes.

Remove the tray from the oven and leave to cool slightly. Add a touch more salt and pepper then serve.

maple roasted sweet potato wedges

SERVES 4

2 large sweet potatoes, washed and trimmed
3 tbsp olive oil
Pinch of flaked sea salt
2 tbsp maple syrup

Preheat the oven to 200°c.

Cut the sweet potatoes into quarters to form thick evenly-sized wedges. Place the wedges onto a lined baking tray, skin side up, and brush them with olive oil using a silicone brush. Sprinkle with salt.

Place the tray in the preheated oven and leave them to cook for 20 minutes, then remove and brush with the maple syrup. Place back in the oven for a further 5 minutes before serving.

roast potatoes

SERVES 6

1kg potatoes, peeled and halved
(or quartered if large)
50g butter
3 tbsp olive oil
1 head of garlic, cloves separated, skin on
20g fresh rosemary
Pinch of flaked sea salt
Grind of black pepper

Preheat your oven to 200°c.

Place the potatoes into a large saucepan of salted water over a high heat, cover and bring to the boil. Reduce the heat to medium and cook for 8 to 10 minutes or until just tender. Drain well and return to the saucepan. Cover and shake the pan to fluff the edges of the potatoes.

Put the butter and oil in a large roasting tin and heat in the oven for 5 minutes. Add the potatoes, garlic and rosemary leaves to the tin, turn them in the butter and oil and give the tin a shake so they are all well coated. Season generously with salt and pepper.

Roast the potatoes in the preheated oven for 50 to 60 minutes, turning every 20 minutes, or until the potatoes are golden and crunchy.

miso black beans, mushrooms & spinach

SERVES 4

2 tbsp sunflower oil
200g shiitake mushrooms, sliced
1cm fresh ginger, peeled and grated
2 cloves of garlic, peeled and grated
2 spring onions, thinly sliced (white part only)
50ml vegetable stock
2 tbsp brown rice miso paste
400g tinned black beans, drained and rinsed
Handful of baby spinach
Pinch of flaked sea salt
Grind of black pepper
Sesame seeds
Togarashi

In a non-stick frying pan, heat half of the sunflower oil over a medium heat. Add the mushrooms and cook for a few minutes until they get some colour, then transfer them to a plate.

Add the rest of the oil with the ginger, garlic and spring onion. Cook for 2 minutes until softened, then add the vegetable stock and mix well.

Mix the miso paste with two tablespoons of water then add it to the pan, introduce the mushrooms back in and cook for 2 minutes.

Add the black beans and spinach, then stir well until coated and all the spinach has just wilted. Season with salt and pepper, then serve with sesame seeds and togarashi for sprinkling over the top.

soy and garlic broccoli and pak choi

SERVES 4

1 tbsp sunflower oil
2 cloves of garlic, peeled and sliced
1 shallot, peeled and sliced
½ red bird's eye chilli, deseeded and sliced
2cm fresh ginger, peeled and grated
200g tenderstem broccoli, stalks trimmed
200g pak choi, base removed and leaves separated
1 tbsp soy sauce
1 tsp sesame oil

Heat the sunflower oil in a large frying pan over a medium heat, add the garlic, shallot, chilli and ginger to the pan and fry for 1 to 2 minutes.

Next add the broccoli along with a splash of water to help steam it, then fry it quickly for around 2 minutes.

Add the pak choi and then cover the pan with a lid for 30 seconds to help wilt the leaves. Add the soy sauce and sesame oil and coat the greens well in the sauce. Serve immediately.

miso aubergines

SERVES 4

2 medium aubergines
2 tbsp sunflower oil
3 tbsp brown rice miso
3 tbsp honey or maple syrup
2 tbsp soy sauce
2 tsp sesame oil
1 tsp sesame seeds, toasted
1 spring onion, sliced (white part only)
Handful of fresh coriander

Preheat the oven to 180°c.

Halve the aubergines lengthways and score the flesh with a sharp knife in a criss-cross pattern.

Heat half of the oil in a frying pan and cook the aubergines, flesh-side down, for 5 minutes, then flip and cook for 5 more minutes.

Make a paste with the brown rice miso, honey or syrup, soy sauce, sesame oil and the remaining tablespoon of sunflower oil.

Transfer the aubergines to a roasting tin, drizzle the paste over them and then roast them in the preheated oven for 20 minutes. Keep an eye on them to make sure the tops don't catch and burn.

Sprinkle the miso aubergines with toasted sesame seeds, sliced spring onion and coriander to serve.

spicy miso corn on the cob

SERVES 4

4 fresh cobs of corn, shucked
50g unsalted butter, at room temperature
50g white miso paste

For the topping
5g fresh chives, finely chopped
1 tsp togarashi (optional)
Pinch of flaked sea salt
1 lime, cut into wedges

Drop the cobs of corn into a large saucepan of boiling salted water and cook for 5 minutes.

In a small bowl, mix the butter and miso paste together. Drain your corn and immediately brush the cobs all over with the miso butter mixture.

For the topping

Sprinkle with the chives, togarashi (if using) and salt, then serve the dressed corn with lime wedges.

Dressings, Dips & Staples

Here I share with you all of my dips and dressings, which are all really versatile and can be enjoyed with specific dishes or just as an accompaniment. I've also included some 'go-to' staples, like gravy and even bread rolls, which will enhance and work with so many dishes within this book.

french dressing

1 tbsp white wine vinegar
1 tsp Dijon mustard
3 tbsp olive oil
1 clove of garlic, peeled and grated
Pinch of flaked sea salt
Grind of black pepper

Put all the ingredients into a jar or bowl and shake or whisk until well combined.

Store in an airtight container in the fridge for up to 1 week.

honey and lemon dressing

4 tbsp olive oil
4 tbsp lemon juice
4 tbsp runny honey
Pinch of flaked sea salt
Grind of black pepper

Put all the ingredients into a jar or bowl and shake or whisk until well combined.

Store in an airtight container in the fridge for up to 1 week.

maple and tahini dressing

10 tbsp tahini
4 tbsp maple syrup
2 tbsp lemon juice
5 tbsp hot water

Put all the ingredients into blender or food processor and blend until well combined. Add more hot water to thin further if preferred.

Store in an airtight container in the fridge for up to 1 week.

pomegranate dressing

5 tbsp pomegranate molasses
3 tbsp olive oil
2 tsp balsamic vinegar
2 cloves of garlic, peeled and grated
¼ tsp ground cinnamon
¼ tsp ground nutmeg

Put all the ingredients into a jar or bowl and shake or whisk until well combined.

Store in an airtight container in the fridge for up to 1 week.

caesar dressing

20g Parmesan block
4 anchovy fillets, finely chopped
4 tbsp Greek yoghurt
2 tbsp mayonnaise
1 clove of garlic, peeled and sliced
1 tsp olive oil
¼ lemon, zested and juiced
Pinch of flaked sea salt
Grind of black pepper

Blitz the Parmesan in the food processor until it resembles fine breadcrumbs. Add all the remaining ingredients, then blitz everything together until the anchovies and garlic have been finely chopped. Taste the dressing and add seasoning if needed.

Store in an airtight container in the fridge for up to 1 week.

vegan caesar dressing

150g cashews, soaked in water overnight
100ml almond milk
2 tbsp hot water
1 tbsp lemon juice
2 tsp garlic powder
1 tbsp nutritional yeast
Pinch of flaked sea salt
Grind of black pepper

Drain and rinse the cashews, discarding the soaking water, then place them into the blender with all the other ingredients and whizz until smooth.

Store in an airtight container in the fridge for up to 1 week.

tamarind dressing

300ml water
2 tbsp tamarind paste
2 tbsp palm sugar, grated
1 tbsp soy sauce

In a medium saucepan, combine the water, tamarind paste, palm sugar and soy sauce. Bring to the boil then lower the heat to a simmer for a few minutes until the liquid starts to reduce and turns glossy. Stir well and then set aside to cool completely.

Store in an airtight container in the fridge for up to 1 week.

mayonnaise

1 egg
1 tbsp lemon juice
1 tsp Dijon mustard
250ml sunflower oil
Pinch of flaked sea salt
Pinch of ground white pepper
Clove of garlic (optional)

Place the egg, lemon juice and mustard into your blender or food processor. Pour the oil in slowly and blend until the mixture is thick and creamy and all the oil has been incorporated. Add salt and pepper to taste and stir through.

Store in an airtight container in the fridge for up to 1 week.

To make aioli

Simply add one peeled and grated clove of garlic to the above before the oil.

vegan mayonnaise

50ml aquafaba (the liquid from a jar of cooked chickpeas)
1 tsp lemon juice
½ tsp Dijon mustard
150ml sunflower oil
Pinch of flaked sea salt
Pinch of ground white pepper
Clove of garlic (optional)

Place the aquafaba, lemon juice and mustard into your blender or food processor. Start blending, pour the oil in slowly and continue to blend until the mixture is thick and creamy and all the oil has been incorporated. Add salt and pepper to taste and stir through.

Store in an airtight container in the fridge for up to 1 week.

To make vegan aioli

Simply add one peeled and grated clove of garlic to the above before the oil.

tomato ketchup

300g tomato purée
100g chopped tinned tomatoes
100g maple syrup
20ml white wine vinegar
8 tbsp hot water
1 tbsp onion powder
1 tsp garlic powder
1 tsp flaked sea salt
½ tsp ground cinnamon
Grind of black pepper

Place all the ingredients into your blender or food processor and blend well. Place into the saucepan over a medium heat and simmer for a few minutes. Leave to cool.

Store in an airtight container in the fridge for up to 1 week.

bbq sauce

55g coconut sugar
50ml soy sauce
300ml tomato ketchup (see above)
Pinch of flaked sea salt
Grind of black pepper

Put the coconut sugar, soy sauce and tomato ketchup into a small saucepan over a medium heat and season with salt and pepper. Simmer for a few minutes to combine the flavours and ensure the sugar has dissolved.

Store in an airtight container in the fridge for up to 1 week.

raita

2 tsp olive oil
1 clove of garlic, peeled and grated
1cm fresh ginger, peeled and grated
½ tsp garam masala
200g cucumber, deseeded and grated
½ tsp fine salt
10g fresh mint leaves, finely chopped
10g fresh coriander leaves, finely chopped
250g Greek or coconut yoghurt
½ lemon, zested and juiced
Pinch of flaked sea salt
Grind of black pepper

Heat the oil in a small saucepan over a low heat. Add the garlic, ginger and garam masala and cook for 1 minute, then place in a bowl to cool and set aside.

Place the cucumber and salt in a colander for 10 minutes. The excess liquid should come out of the cucumber. Pat dry with kitchen paper, then add to the bowl along with the mint, coriander, yoghurt, lemon zest and juice. Season the raita well and then serve.

satay sauce

1 tbsp green Thai paste (optional)
100g peanut butter
50ml coconut milk
5 tbsp water
2 tsp soy sauce
1 tbsp coconut sugar
1 tbsp lime juice

In a small saucepan over a low heat, combine the Thai paste, peanut butter, coconut milk, water, soy sauce and sugar. Mix well until the sugar has dissolved and everything is well combined, then allow the sauce to simmer and thicken. Remove from the heat, add the lime juice and stir again.

Store in an airtight container in the fridge for up to 1 week.

almond butter dipping sauce

5 tbsp almond butter
1 clove of garlic, peeled and chopped
1cm fresh ginger, peeled and chopped
1 tbsp soy sauce
1 tbsp lime juice
1 tbsp maple syrup
2 tbsp hot water

Add all your ingredients to a blender or food processor. Blend well, and add more hot water to thin if preferred.

Store in an airtight container in the fridge for up to 1 week.

gyoza dipping sauce

50ml rice vinegar
50ml soy sauce
1 clove of garlic, peeled and grated
1 tsp fresh ginger, peeled and grated
1 tsp sesame oil
⅛ tsp dried chilli flakes

Add all the ingredients to a bowl, stir well and then set aside for the flavours to develop before serving.

Store in an airtight container in the fridge for up to 1 week.

tomato pasta sauce

1 medium onion, chopped
2 cloves of garlic, peeled and sliced
1 tbsp sunflower oil
1kg fresh ripe tomatoes, or 800g tinned chopped tomatoes
1 tbsp red wine vinegar
1 tbsp olive oil
Pinch of flaked sea salt
Grind of black pepper

In a saucepan over a medium heat, cook the onion and garlic in the sunflower oil for 3 minutes until softened and translucent. Add the fresh or tinned tomatoes and red wine vinegar, then cook for a further 10 minutes. Remove the pan from the heat, then leave to cool.

Add the tomato sauce to a blender with the olive oil, salt and pepper. Blend well until smooth.

Store in an airtight container in the fridge for up to 1 week.

vegan carbonara sauce

150g cashews, soaked in water overnight
100ml almond milk
50ml vegetable stock
2 tbsp nutritional yeast
Pinch of flaked sea salt
Grind of black pepper

Drain and rinse the cashews, discarding the soaking water, then add them to the blender with all the remaining ingredients and whizz until smooth. Warm through in a saucepan over a medium heat and use as normal with your pasta.

Store in an airtight container in the fridge for up to 1 week.

vegan parmesan

200g cashews
4 tbsp nutritional yeast
1 tsp Himalayan salt
1 tsp garlic powder

Add all the ingredients to a food processor and blend until whizzed into a breadcrumb-like texture.

Store in an airtight container in the fridge for up to 2 weeks.

pesto

150g Parmesan block
40g pine nuts
150g fresh basil
1 clove of garlic, peeled and roughly chopped
4 tbsp olive oil
Pinch of flaked sea salt
Grind of black pepper

Chop your Parmesan into chunks. Toast your pine nuts in a dry pan over a medium heat, being careful not to let them burn as they can turn quickly. Set aside to cool. In a food processor, add the Parmesan and whizz into breadcrumb-sized pieces, then add the rest of the ingredients, including the toasted pine nuts, and blend until the pesto is your preferred texture.

tamarind dipping sauce

100ml tamarind paste
250ml warm water
4 tbsp coconut sugar
½ tsp ground cumin
½ tsp chilli powder
½ tsp ground ginger
5 tbsp soy sauce

Add the tamarind paste, water and coconut sugar to your saucepan over a medium heat. Stir until the coconut sugar has dissolved. Add the cumin, chilli, ginger and soy sauce.

Stir well until the mixture thickens, allow it to come to the boil and then remove from the heat. Leave to cool before serving.

Store in an airtight container in the fridge for up to 1 week.

spice rub

1 tsp Himalayan salt
1 tsp ground coriander
1 tbsp onion powder
1 tsp garlic powder
1 tsp smoked paprika
1 tsp ground cumin
½ tsp cayenne pepper
Grind of black pepper
¼ tsp dried chilli flakes
¼ tsp dried parsley
2 tbsp coconut sugar

This recipe makes 100g which is enough to use as one serving for any meat or fish.

Pound all the ingredients together using a pestle and mortar until you have a powdery consistency.

Store in an airtight container in the fridge for up to 2 weeks.

gravy

1 tbsp sunflower oil
1 medium onion, peeled and chopped
1 medium carrot, peeled and chopped
1 stick of celery, trimmed and chopped
2 tbsp plain flour
1 fresh bay leaf
2 sprigs of fresh thyme
800ml vegetable, chicken or beef stock
2 tbsp pan drippings (from roasted meat)
1 tsp soy sauce, for darkening (optional)

Put the oil into a large saucepan over a medium heat, then add the onion, carrot and celery. Cook for 5 minutes, then quickly stir in the flour until well combined.

Add the bay leaf, thyme, stock and pan drippings to the vegetables. Stir well, then lower the heat to bring the liquid to a simmer and add the teaspoon of soy sauce, if using. Cook the gravy for 20 minutes to allow the flavours to develop.

Strain the gravy through a sieve into a clean saucepan, and reheat before serving.

thai chilli jam

10 dried red bird's eye chillies
2 tbsp dried shrimp
5 cloves of garlic, peeled and chopped
2 shallots, peeled and chopped
2 tbsp sunflower oil
2 tbsp tamarind paste
1 tbsp fish sauce
80g palm sugar, grated
½ tsp shrimp paste

Toast the dried chillies in a dry frying pan over a medium-high heat until they are just starting to char at the edges. Transfer the chillies to a spice grinder and blend into a fine powder. Set aside.

Place the dried shrimp in the spice grinder and blend until fine and fluffy.

Place the garlic and shallots into your food processor and process until a paste forms, then add the chilli and dried shrimp powders and process again to combine.

Heat the oil in a large non-stick frying pan over a medium heat and add the paste. Cook and stir for approximately 8 to 10 minutes or until just starting to caramelise.

In a small bowl, mix the tamarind, fish sauce, palm sugar and shrimp paste. Add this to the pan and stir until all the ingredients are well combined and the sugar has dissolved.

Cook the jam for a further 2 to 5 minutes until the mixture is a deep dark colour and sticky.

Store in an airtight container in the fridge for up to 2 weeks.

pineapple chutney

1 large pineapple, peeled, cored and diced into 1cm cubes
3 tbsp coconut oil
1 tsp dried chilli flakes
1 cinnamon stick
½ tsp ground turmeric
4 cardamom pods
600ml water
150g palm sugar, grated
½ tsp flaked sea salt

Peel, core and dice the pineapple so you have 1cm cubes.

Melt the coconut oil in a pan on a medium heat, then heat the chilli, cinnamon, turmeric and cardamom pods for a minute, stirring them constantly to avoid the spices catching.

Add the water, palm sugar and salt to the pan. Stir until the sugar has dissolved then add the diced pineapple. Give the mixture a good stir, then place a lid on the pan and turn the heat down to low. Simmer for 40 to 60 minutes until the pineapple is cooked through and the liquid is syrupy.

Store in an airtight container in the fridge for up to 2 weeks.

chilli tomato chutney

500g tomatoes
4 cloves of garlic, peeled
1 red bird's eye chilli, finely chopped
2½cm fresh ginger, peeled and roughly sliced
150g palm sugar, grated
2 tbsp fish sauce (optional)
100ml malt vinegar

Blitz the tomatoes with the garlic, chilli and ginger in a food processor. Pour the mixture into a saucepan then add the sugar, fish sauce (if using) and vinegar.

Bring to the boil, stirring slowly. Reduce to a simmer and cook for 30 to 40 minutes, stirring from time to time. The mixture will turn darker and sticky. Keep an eye on the chutney so you don't allow it to catch and burn.

Store in an airtight container in the fridge for up to 2 weeks.

almond milk

MAKES 800ML

This almond milk is just gorgeous. You can enjoy it on its own or in your hot drinks, and you can use it to make your chia pudding and overnight oats too. It's creamy and so very good. I love it with the addition of Medjool dates and vanilla but you can omit them for a less sweet version. This needs to be cold to be enjoyed properly.

350g almonds, soaked in water overnight
2 Medjool dates, pitted (optional)
Pinch of Himalayan salt
750ml filtered water
½ tsp vanilla powder (optional)

Drain and rinse the almonds, discarding the soaking water.

Add them to the blender with the dates (if using), salt and filtered water then blend well for 3 to 4 minutes until smooth.

Strain the milk through a nut bag or muslin cloth over a bowl and squeeze firmly to force all the liquid through.

Stir the vanilla (if using) into the milk, then store in the fridge in a glass bottle for up to 3 days. Shake well before using.

coconut milk

MAKES 800ML

This milk is magic; once you try it and see just how easy it is to make, you most likely won't ever want the carton stuff again. The dates are optional, but they sweeten it nicely and make it just so delicious. This needs to be cold to be enjoyed properly, so make sure you place it in the fridge until chilled before using.

150g flaked coconut
2 Medjool dates, pitted (optional)
750ml filtered water
Pinch of Himalayan salt

Add the coconut to the blender with the dates (if using), water and salt, then blend well for 3 to 4 minutes until smooth.

Strain the milk through a nut bag or muslin cloth over a bowl and squeeze firmly to force all the liquid through.

Store in the fridge in a glass bottle for up to 3 days. Shake well before using.

bread rolls

MAKES 10

675g tipo 00 flour, plus extra for dusting
7g dried yeast
2 tsp salt
1 tbsp olive oil
580ml warm water

Place all the ingredients in a large bowl and mix to form a wet, sticky dough. Cover the bowl with a damp tea towel and allow the dough to stand for 2 hours. It will double in size and form large bubbles.

Flour your work surface well, turn the proved dough out and knead for a few minutes, then divide it into ten equal pieces and shape these into balls.

Take a Dutch oven or casserole dish with a lid and lightly dust with the flour. Place the rolls inside, loosely cover the pan with lightly oiled cling film and leave to stand for 30 minutes or until the dough has doubled in size again. Meanwhile, preheat your oven to 220°c.

Remove the cling film, place the lid on top and bake the rolls for 20 minutes. Remove the lid and cook for a further 20 minutes, or until the crusts are brown. Carefully lift them out and allow the rolls to cool completely on a wire rack.

plain rice

350g jasmine or basmati rice
500ml water
Pinch of flaked sea salt

Put the rice in a sieve and rinse it under the tap with cold water. Place the washed rice, water and a pinch of salt into a saucepan over a medium heat and bring to the boil.

Reduce the heat and cover the pan with a lid. Cook the rice for 12 minutes until tender, then take the pan off the heat without removing the lid and allow the rice to steam for 5 minutes. Add an extra pinch of salt and fluff up the rice with a fork before serving.

If you are cooking brown rice, it will need a far longer cooking time of 20 to 25 minutes, and 8 minutes steaming.

coconut rice

350g jasmine rice
400ml tinned coconut milk, shaken well before opening
500ml water
2 kaffir lime leaves
Pinch of flaked sea salt

Put the rice in a sieve and rinse it under the tap with cold water.

Place the washed rice, coconut milk, water, lime leaves and a pinch of salt into a medium saucepan over a high heat.

Bring to the boil, then reduce the heat to low, cover the pan with a lid and cook the rice for 14 minutes until sticky and creamy. Stir well then remove from the heat.

Allow the rice to stand, covered, for 5 minutes. Remove the lime leaves, and stir through an extra pinch of salt before serving.

soft boiled eggs

4 large free-range eggs

Bring a large saucepan of water to the boil over a medium to high heat.

Carefully lower your eggs into the water using a slotted spoon. Set a timer. Cook your eggs for the desired cooking time, maintaining a gentle boil. I find that boiling the eggs for 6 minutes gives you a completely runny yolk, and 6 minutes 30 seconds for a runny yolk with a firm edge.

On the same note, if you prefer to have hard boiled eggs, then let them boil for 10 minutes.

Once time is up, transfer your eggs straight to an ice bath and chill until they are just slightly warm: about 2 minutes. This stops the eggs from cooking further and leaving a grey lining around the yolk, and it also makes them far easier to peel when cool.

Remove the cooled eggs, crack them all over and peel gently, starting from the fattest end containing the air pocket.

Eat immediately, or refrigerate if not using right away.

Guilt-free indulgence

My final chapters are all about the sweet stuff. As a parent, it horrified me seeing the impact that refined sugar had on my boys, turning them from little angels into wild eyed children, stomping their feet or screaming on the floor, demanding more. Using coconut sugar or maple syrup means they get the slight 'up' from the natural sugar, but not the high spike that comes from the refined stuff, accompanied by a massive drop.

I am also very conscious of what goes inside my own body; I don't want a ton of butter in my cakes, as it's just not healthy. My cakes taste like they have butter in, but they don't. I think you'll be surprised.

Being a mother is what started this for me, not just realising the impact refined sugar can have, but seeing the difference in both myself and my boys whenever we had it too. As I get older, I know that I can't just eat whatever I want. I see the effects of certain foods on my body much more noticeably, particularly in where weight now tends to stick and is so much harder to lose again.

As with all foods, moderation is still just as important, as is portion control, but all of my recipes satisfy that need for a sweet fix, and you'll even gain health benefits from them.

So I set out on a mission to adapt all my recipes in order to make them refined sugar-free, but still taste just the same as the original versions. So many of my deli customers were asking for 'made-without' options by then, so by removing the gluten, eggs and dairy, I could make my recipes accessible for everyone, no matter what their dietary requirements.

I've created them from a non-vegan, chef, foodie and mummy palate, making healthy desserts that taste amazing. Natural sugars are a healthier option, so I use local honey, coconut sugar, pure maple syrup and brown rice syrup.

As with all foods, moderation is still just as important, as is portion control, but all of my recipes satisfy that need for a sweet fix, and you'll even gain health benefits from them.

All my experimenting and playing around with recipes made me fall head over heels in love with making sweet treats, both raw and baked, just using plants, meaning they are so much healthier for you, and of course, completely guilt-free.

precise with the ratio of one tablespoon of ground flaxseed or chia seeds to three tablespoons of warm water is essential.

I place tins of good quality full-fat coconut milk in the fridge to use for many recipes. This is to firm the contents of the tins up and then to use only the thickened creamy part from the top.

When making chocolate, working quickly to mix everything together is key. Once it hits the cold air it will set, so if your kitchen is cold, you will need to work fast.

Raw is a plant-based way to prepare food in which ingredients are not heated past a certain temperature, maintaining their integrity and nutritional value.

I use a Vitamix for making my cheesecake filling because it makes it so very smooth and creamy. However, a normal blender works well too; you will just need to let it run long enough. You can keep all the raw sweet bites, tarts and cheesecakes in the freezer, and cut off little bites to enjoy whenever you need a sweet fix to pick you up throughout the day.

With my bakes, just like in all baking recipes, it's a science, so ensuring that everything is measured accurately is very important. Take care to work through the measurements and the method, step by step, to ensure a perfect outcome every time.

You may find, to begin with, that you need to stock up with a lot of new ingredients, which I know can all add up. But once you adapt to stocking your cupboards with these ingredients, you'll find that the investment in your body and your health far outweighs the cost.

Once you've tried these recipes, you'll really notice a difference in your palate when it comes to your cravings for sweet treats. My guilt-free desserts will completely satisfy them, leaving you perfectly happy and not needing anything else.

You'll be swapping out butter for coconut oil, cream cheese for cashews, biscuits for nuts, making your own chocolate using cacao powder and maple syrup, and using Medjool dates and nut butter to make the most delicious and rich caramels.

There are several points to cover for these chapters to help you to understand them better before you dive in. My sweet bites, tarts and cheesecakes are all naturally gluten-free, and all the bakes have been tested with gluten-free flour. They all work like-for-like so you can simply swap the flours and baking agents over. The same applies when using oats.

Raw is a plant-based way to prepare food in which ingredients are not heated past a certain temperature, maintaining their integrity and nutritional value. The important things to remember when making the cheesecakes are to soak your cashews overnight so that they really plump up, and to rinse them well. This is what forms the basis of your cheesecake.

Melted cacao butter always needs to be poured in last, as it firms up very quickly when it touches cold ingredients or containers.

Understanding the egg replacements is very important. Ensure you allow them time to sit and absorb the water in a small bowl because they need to thicken in order to work properly. Being

Sweet Bites

energy balls

MAKES 15

Energy balls are mega easy to make and so very satisfying. I keep these in my freezer for when I'm having a slump in my day and need to feel more energised, or simply a sweet fix. My boys absolutely love them, and they make great snacks for their school bags too. Here are six flavours to choose from.

Almond

50g jumbo rolled oats
150g almonds
300g Medjool dates, pitted
2 tbsp coconut oil, melted
2 tbsp almond butter
Pinch of Himalayan salt

Place the oats and almonds into a food processor and whizz until they form a chunky flour, then add the remaining ingredients and blend everything until well combined.

Roll the mixture into 15 balls. Refrigerate the energy balls until ready to serve, or freeze and take out 10 minutes before serving.

Chocolate Chia

100g almonds
300g Medjool dates, pitted
20g cacao powder
1 tbsp chia seeds
2 tbsp coconut oil, melted
1 tbsp almond butter
Pinch of Himalayan salt

Place the almonds into the food processor and whizz until finely chopped, then add the remaining ingredients and blend everything until well combined.

Roll the mixture into 15 balls. Refrigerate the energy balls until ready to serve, or freeze and take out 10 minutes before serving.

Ginger

100g jumbo rolled oats
100g almonds
200g Medjool dates, pitted
2 tsp ground ginger
1 tsp fresh ginger, grated
Pinch of Himalayan salt
2 tbsp coconut oil, melted
5 tbsp brown rice syrup or maple syrup

Place the oats and almonds into a food processor and whizz until they form a chunky flour, then add the remaining ingredients and blend everything until well combined.

Roll the mixture into 15 balls. Refrigerate the energy balls until ready to serve, or freeze and take out 10 minutes before serving.

Peanut Butter

160g almonds
100g peanuts
3 tbsp smooth peanut butter
40g buckwheat
300g Medjool dates, pitted
¼ tsp vanilla powder
1 tbsp brown rice syrup or maple syrup
⅛ tsp Himalayan salt

Place the almonds and peanuts into the food processor and whizz until finely chopped, then add the remaining ingredients and blend everything until well combined.

Roll the mixture into 15 balls. Refrigerate the energy balls until ready to serve, or freeze and take out 10 minutes before serving.

Carrot Cake

400g pecans
50g almonds
200g Medjool dates, pitted
120g carrot, peeled and grated
1 tbsp almond butter
1 tbsp brown rice syrup or maple syrup
1 tsp ground cinnamon
½ tsp ground nutmeg
½ tsp ground ginger
⅛ tsp Himalayan salt

Make the pecan coating first. Put 100g of the pecans into the food processor and pulse until finely chopped, then transfer into a small bowl and set aside.

Next add the remaining 300g of pecans and the almonds to the food processor. Pulse until they are all finely chopped, then add all the remaining ingredients and blend until everything is well combined. Roll the mixture into 15 balls and coat them with the crushed pecans.

Refrigerate until ready to serve, or freeze and take out 10 minutes before serving.

Matcha and Pistachio

140g almonds
70g pistachios
40g desiccated coconut
1½ tbsp matcha powder
¼ tsp vanilla powder
300g Medjool dates, pitted
½ tbsp brown rice syrup or maple syrup
1 tbsp tahini

Place the almonds and pistachios into the food processor and whizz until finely chopped, then add the remaining ingredients and blend everything until well combined.

Roll the mixture into 15 balls. Refrigerate the energy balls until ready to serve, or freeze and take out 10 minutes before serving.

fudge

Growing up in Cornwall, there were always many fudge shops around. As an adult, I love fudge and it was on my original mymuybueno Deli menu too, but all that sugar and butter is just no good for you. This tastes just as satisfying, and you can enjoy more than one piece without the sickly feeling after. It's the perfect dose for a small sweet fix.

300g Medjool dates, pitted
5 tbsp almond butter
2 tbsp coconut butter
1 tbsp coconut oil, melted
2 tbsp cacao powder
¼ tsp vanilla powder
Pinch of Himalayan salt

Place all the ingredients into a food processor and whizz until everything is combined and the mixture is smooth.

Line a small rectangular tin with parchment paper and pour the fudge mix in. If your tin isn't quite the right size, just push the mixture to one end and make sure the fudge is about 2cm deep.

Place the fudge in the freezer for 2 hours until solid, then chop it into 2cm by 2cm pieces. Separate these, place them back in the freezer and take out 5 minutes before serving.

billionaire's shortbread

MAKES 9

This recipe is a nod towards super yachts and their owners, the clientele I work with a lot in my agencies. They aren't just rich, they're really, really rich. This is a decadent and delicious wedge of nutty shortbread-like biscuit, layered with gooey caramel, topped with chocolate.

For the base

150g almonds
120g pecans
200g Medjool dates, pitted
2 tbsp almond butter

For the caramel

300g Medjool dates, pitted
140g almond butter
50g brown rice syrup or maple syrup
2 tbsp coconut oil, melted
¼ tsp vanilla powder
Pinch of Himalayan salt

For the chocolate glaze

100ml coconut oil, melted
60g cacao powder
50g maple syrup

For the base

Line a 20cm square tin with parchment paper. Place the almonds and pecans into a food processor and blend for a minute until broken down into a 'wet sand' consistency.

Add the dates and almond butter then blend well until the mixture becomes sticky and all the dates have broken down.

Press the biscuit mixture into the tin, pushing it down firmly with a spatula to create an even, level surface before placing the tin into the freezer.

For the caramel

Next, make the caramel layer. Place all the ingredients into your food processor and blend until smooth and creamy, then pour the caramel onto the chilled biscuit layer.

Put the tray back into the freezer for about 1 hour so that the caramel becomes firm enough to pour the chocolate glaze over.

For the chocolate glaze

Whisk all the ingredients together in a bowl. Use the glaze immediately, pouring it over the set caramel layer. Freeze the billionaire's shortbread again once the glaze is on, then cut into 3cm by 3cm squares when set. Indulge and enjoy.

chocolate caramel biscuit bars

MAKES 12

These childhood treats take you back with that classic combination of biscuit, caramel and chocolate. When you fancy some chocolate, these really do the job well. Everyone loves them, and so will you.

For the biscuit base
100g macadamias
100g jumbo rolled oats
2 tbsp brown rice syrup or maple syrup
2 tbsp coconut oil, melted
½ tsp vanilla powder
Pinch of Himalayan salt

For the caramel
200g Medjool dates, pitted
3 tbsp almond butter
3 tbsp water
¼ tsp vanilla powder
Pinch of Himalayan salt

For the chocolate glaze
100ml coconut oil, melted
60g cacao powder
50g maple syrup

For the biscuit base

Place the macadamia nuts and oats into the food processor. Blend until they have broken down to a flour, then add the remaining ingredients and process until well incorporated.

Line a small rectangular tin with parchment paper and press the biscuit base into it. If your tin isn't quite the right size, just push the mixture to one end and make sure the biscuit is about half a centimetre deep. Place in the freezer to firm up while you make the caramel.

For the caramel

Place all the ingredients into your blender and process until smooth. If it's still quite thick, just add another tablespoon of water. Spread your caramel over the frozen biscuit base and pop the tin back in the freezer for another hour.

Remove the tin from the freezer and carefully lift your caramel topped biscuit out. Remove the parchment paper and place on a chopping board. Working quickly, cut the caramel biscuit in half, and then cut each half lengthways into long rectangular bars and place back into the freezer.

For the chocolate glaze

Whisk all the ingredients together in a bowl and use the glaze immediately. Spread a clean sheet of baking paper on a tray. Dip each bar into the chocolate glaze to cover them liberally all over, gently shake off any excess and place them onto the lined tray, making sure they are the right way up with the biscuit on the bottom.

Store the chocolate caramel biscuit bars in the freezer to allow the chocolate glaze to harden. Eat within 5 to 10 minutes of removing them from the freezer. Enjoy.

mint chocolate squares

MAKES 18 BITE-SIZE SQUARES

Growing up, I used to love chocolate mints after dinner. This recipe is inspired by those and serves the same purpose, but you can indulge with these at any time of day.

For the base
110g pecans
80g buckwheat
40g cacao powder
¼ tsp vanilla powder
100g Medjool dates, pitted
60g brown rice syrup or maple syrup

For the peppermint filling
250g cashews, soaked in water overnight
100g brown rice syrup or maple syrup
50ml water
2 tsp peppermint extract
100g cacao butter

For the chocolate glaze
100ml coconut oil, melted
60g cacao powder
50g maple syrup
6 mint leaves, finely sliced and stems removed

For the base
Line a 20cm square tin with parchment paper. First reduce the pecans to small pieces in the food processor. Add the buckwheat, cacao powder and vanilla then pulse to combine. Add the dates and brown rice syrup or maple syrup then process until the mixture is well combined and sticky.

Press the mixture into the tin, pushing it down firmly with a spatula to create an even, level surface before placing the tin into the freezer.

For the peppermint filling
Drain and rinse the cashews, discarding the soaking water, then add them to your processor with the syrup, water and peppermint and blend well. Melt your cacao butter in a saucepan until it has become liquid. Add this in last and continue to blend well until the mixture is smooth and creamy.

Pour the peppermint filling over the base then put the tin in the freezer for a few hours until both the layers are solid.

For the chocolate glaze
Meanwhile, make the chocolate glaze. Whisk all the ingredients except the mint leaves together in a bowl, then use the glaze immediately by pouring it over the set peppermint filling.

Leave to freeze in the tin overnight, and then cut into small squares before serving. Top with the fresh sliced mint leaves.

chia cinnamon doughnuts

MAKES 8

These are made the same way as energy balls, and I actually prefer eating these when they are quite hard, straight from the freezer. If you are not a huge fan of cinnamon, you can simply take this out and use vanilla or maca powder instead.

For the doughnuts
170g jumbo rolled oats
85g desiccated coconut
200g Medjool dates, pitted
2 tbsp coconut oil, melted
100g brown rice syrup or maple syrup
2 tbsp almond butter
4 tbsp chia seeds
1 tbsp psyllium husk
2½ tsp ground cinnamon
Pinch of Himalayan salt

For the chocolate glaze
100ml coconut oil, melted
60g cacao powder
50g maple syrup

For the doughnuts

You will need a small silicone doughnut mould for this recipe.

Place your oats into the food processor and process well to break them down into a flour.

Add all your remaining doughnut ingredients and blend until well combined. Roll the mixture into sausages and press these firmly into the moulds. Place the doughnuts in the freezer for 2 hours.

For the chocolate glaze

Whisk all the ingredients together in a bowl, then use the glaze immediately. Pop the doughnuts out of their moulds and onto a wire rack, with parchment paper lining the surface underneath. Using a spoon, drizzle the glaze over the doughnuts in a back and forth motion across the top, or use a small piping bag for better accuracy. Put them back into the freezer to firm up for at least an hour. Enjoy.

vanilla doughnuts

MAKES 8

I love making these, a variation on energy balls. Delicious small raw doughnuts will boost your day, and satisfy any sweet cravings you have.

For the doughnuts

240g jumbo rolled oats, weighed out into 80g and 160g bowls
150g cashews, soaked in water overnight
200g Medjool dates, pitted
2 tbsp maple or brown rice syrup
1 tbsp psyllium husk
½ tsp vanilla powder
Pinch of Himalayan salt

For the vanilla glaze

200g coconut butter
¼ tsp vanilla powder

For the doughnuts

You will need a small silicone doughnut mould for this recipe.

First, put the 80g of rolled oats into a food processor and blend them into a flour. Drain and rinse the cashews, discarding the soaking water, then add them to the oat flour with all your remaining doughnut ingredients, and blend until a moist dough forms.

Roll the mixture into sausages and then firmly press them into the moulds. Place the doughnuts in the freezer for 2 hours to set.

For the vanilla glaze

Put the coconut butter in a saucepan on a low heat and warm for just long enough to let it melt and become glossy. Remove the pan from the heat and stir the vanilla into the butter.

Pop the doughnuts out of their moulds and onto a wire rack, with parchment paper lining the surface underneath.

Dunk each of your doughnuts into the glaze top down, twist and pull out gently. You will need to repeat this step to get a thick enough glaze. Time is of the essence to do this before your glaze hardens, so work fast to glaze all your doughnuts.

Keep them in the freezer and take out 10 minutes before serving.

chocolate coconut balls

This recipe takes you back to your childhood once again, with these perfect retro chocolate and coconut balls. They are not too sweet but satisfy those cravings.

For the balls
85g cashews, soaked in water overnight
40ml tinned coconut milk,
refrigerated overnight
115g desiccated coconut
3 tbsp coconut oil, melted
1 tbsp coconut butter
60g brown rice syrup or maple syrup

For the chocolate glaze
100ml coconut oil, melted
60g cacao powder
50g maple syrup

Do not shake the tin of coconut milk, just remove it from the fridge, open and gently scrape 40g of the thick coconut cream off the top. Put this into your food processor. Drain and rinse the soaked cashews, discarding the soaking water, then add these and all the remaining ingredients to the food processor and blend well.

Weigh and divide the mixture into evenly-sized pieces, then mould them into balls. Carefully insert a toothpick into each ball, then place them on a tray lined with parchment paper. Place in the freezer for around 1 hour.

For the chocolate glaze

Whisk all the ingredients together in a bowl and use the glaze immediately. Once the balls are firm, hold the toothpicks and dip each one into the chocolate glaze, coating them evenly. Wait for the chocolate glaze to firm up like a shell before placing each coated ball back on the tray. Return them to the freezer and then once the chocolate is solid, carefully remove the toothpicks.

Store the chocolate coconut balls in the freezer, and remove them a few minutes before serving. Enjoy.

Bakes

dorset apple cake

This is such a delicious cake, eaten on its own, enjoyed with a cup of tea,
or as a pudding with vanilla nice cream or vanilla whipped cream (p.236).

225g (approx. 3½) Bramley or Granny Smith
apples, peeled, cored and diced

Dry Ingredients
150g ground almonds
160g self-raising flour, sifted
70g coconut sugar, plus 1 tbsp for topping
1 tsp baking powder, sifted
2 tsp ground cinnamon
Pinch of Himalayan salt
100g sultanas

Wet Ingredients
240ml almond milk
120ml sunflower oil
1 tbsp apple cider vinegar

Preheat the oven to 180°c.

Lightly grease a 20cm round cake tin with sunflower oil and line the base with parchment paper.

Place all the dry ingredients except the sultanas into a large mixing bowl and stir them together until there are no lumps. Add the sultanas and diced apples to the bowl, stirring well to coat them in the dry ingredients.

In a separate bowl, mix the wet ingredients together until well combined. Add the wet ingredients to the dry ingredients and stir until everything is well incorporated.

Pour the batter into your prepared tin and gently level it out. Sprinkle over the tablespoon of coconut sugar and bake the cake in the preheated oven on a baking tray for 45 minutes, or until the cake is golden and a toothpick inserted into the middle comes out clean.

Leave in the tin for 10 minutes to cool and then carefully turn the cake out and leave to cool completely on a wire rack.

ginger loaf

SERVES 8

I created this originally with black treacle and golden syrup, to get as close to a Jamaican ginger cake as I could. This is my healthier version, which tastes even more amazing and is sticky thanks to the blackstrap molasses which make it so dense and full of flavour.

For the flax egg
1 tbsp ground flaxseed
3 tbsp warm water

Wet Ingredients
100g coconut oil, slightly softened, plus extra for greasing
65g coconut sugar
200g blackstrap molasses
30ml ginger juice
160ml boiling water

Dry Ingredients
350g self-raising flour
1½ tsp bicarbonate soda
1 tsp baking powder
1½ tsp xanthan gum
2 tsp mixed spice
½ tsp ground ginger
½ tsp Himalayan salt

Preheat the oven to 180°c and grease a 2lb loaf tin lightly with melted coconut oil.

Place the ground flaxseed in a bowl with the warm water, mix well then leave to one side for 10 minutes to thicken up.

Meanwhile, juice the ginger if making your own.

In an electric stand mixer with a paddle attachment, blend the coconut oil with the coconut sugar until the sugar has all dissolved. If you live in a warm place, just pop the oil in the fridge to firm up before mixing, and if it's too solid and hard, allow it to warm slightly to reach a soft butter-like texture so that it will mix well.

Add your flax egg, molasses and ginger juice to the sugar and oil. Mix for a minute until a smooth paste forms. Do not add the hot water just yet.

In a separate bowl, sift together all the dry ingredients. Add this mixture to the wet ingredients and mix well for a few minutes until everything has been incorporated. Now add the boiling water and beat on a low setting until smooth.

Pour the cake mixture into your greased loaf tin and bake for 50 minutes in the preheated oven until a toothpick comes out clean. Leave the cake in the tin for 10 minutes before turning out onto a wire rack to cool completely.

chocolate doughnuts

MAKES 12

These are the moistest and yummiest doughnuts you can imagine. They taste absolutely gorgeous and are always a massive hit with everyone. Don't be afraid of using a piping bag; it's well worth doing as you will have a much neater end result. It's all about control so take your time, don't overfill the bag, and work quickly but carefully.

For the flax egg

2 tbsp ground flaxseed
6 tbsp warm water

Wet Ingredients

290ml almond milk
100ml sunflower oil
1 tsp vanilla paste
1 tbsp espresso

Dry Ingredients

220g self-raising flour, sifted
½ tsp arrowroot, sifted
½ tsp xanthan gum, sifted
45g cacao powder, sifted
½ tsp Himalayan salt
190g coconut sugar

For the chocolate glaze

100ml coconut oil, melted
60g cacao powder
50g maple syrup
Freeze-dried raspberries (optional)

For the doughnuts

You will need a doughnut baking tin for this recipe.

Preheat your oven to 180°c.

Mix the flaxseed with the warm water and leave for 10 minutes to make your flax egg.

In two separate bowls, combine the wet ingredients and then the dry ingredients, except for the coconut sugar.

Stir the flax egg and coconut sugar into the wet ingredients until all the sugar has dissolved, then add this mixture into the dry ingredients and stir until a smooth batter forms.

Transfer your batter into a large piping bag, then pipe it into the doughnut tin and level the tops with a palette knife.

Place the filled doughnut tins onto a baking tray. Bake in the preheated oven for 15 to 20 minutes until well risen, leave to rest in the tin for 10 minutes and then very carefully tease the doughnuts out with a palette knife and your fingers.

Place them onto a wire rack and leave to cool completely.

For the chocolate glaze

While the doughnuts are cooling, make your chocolate glaze. Simply whisk all the ingredients except the freeze-dried raspberries together in a bowl, then use the glaze immediately.

Once your doughnuts are cool, lift them one by one and dip them into the glaze while holding them by the base, which is the exposed part that faced upwards in the moulds. Dip them in straight down, twist and then lift up. Place the glazed doughnuts back on the rack to set before serving. They are lovely sprinkled with freeze-dried raspberries too, if you like.

oat cookies

MAKES 12

These are so quick to make. Using large oats makes all the difference for the crunch and texture. It's a really simple, chunky and delicious cookie.

160g jumbo rolled oats
130g almond butter
100g maple syrup
2 tbsp coconut oil, melted
Pinch of Himalayan salt

Preheat the oven to 180°c and line a large baking tray with parchment paper.

Mix all of the ingredients together in a bowl until they are well combined. Divide the mixture into 12 balls of roughly the same size, place them on the prepared tray and press down gently with wet hands to flatten each one.

Bake the cookies for 10 minutes in the preheated oven until they are golden. Leave for a further 10 minutes to cool and firm up on the tray, then transfer to a wire rack, and leave to cool completely.

chocolate chip cookies

MAKES 12

Everyone loves a good chocolate chip cookie, and this one is simple and delicious. You can make them with either peanut or almond butter, which both work really well.

240g ground almonds
75g plain flour
2 tbsp coconut oil, melted
70g maple syrup
115g almond or peanut butter
Pinch of flaked sea salt
100g cacao paste

Preheat the oven to 180°c and line a baking tray with parchment paper.

Put all of the ingredients except the cacao paste into a bowl and mix until well combined. The cookie dough should be smooth and not look or feel dry.

Chop the cacao paste into small chips and then add them to the bowl. Fold the dough with a spoon to ensure that they are evenly dispersed.

Taking a tablespoon at a time, roll the sticky mixture into even balls with wet hands, working quickly, and then gently flatten each ball on your baking tray.

Place the cookies into the preheated oven and bake for 20 minutes or until golden brown. Leave them on the tray for 10 minutes then transfer to a wire rack so the cookies cool completely.

carrot cake

SERVES 8

I absolutely love carrot cake. Perfect for afternoon tea or any time. The addition of carrot juice
gives it a wonderful colour and incredible moistness.

For the flax egg
1 tbsp ground flaxseed
3 tbsp warm water

Dry Ingredients
280g self-raising flour, sifted
150g coconut sugar
1 tsp each of bicarbonate of soda, baking
powder and arrowroot, sifted
Pinch of Himalayan salt
¼ tsp vanilla powder
2 tsp ground cinnamon
¼ tsp freshly grated nutmeg
50g walnuts, roughly chopped
80g sultanas

Wet Ingredients
290ml carrot juice
150ml sunflower oil
¼ tsp rice wine vinegar
1 orange, zested
140g (approx. 1 large) carrot,
peeled and finely grated
1 tsp fresh ginger, peeled and finely grated

For the buttercream frosting
150g cashews, soaked in water overnight
100ml tinned coconut milk, shaken well
before opening
40ml coconut oil, melted
4 tbsp maple syrup
1 tbsp lemon juice
1 tsp vanilla extract or paste
¼ tsp lemon zest
Pinch of Himalayan salt

To finish
40g walnut halves
1 orange, zested

For the cake
Preheat the oven to 180°c and lightly grease two 20cm sandwich tins
with sunflower oil. Line the bases with parchment paper.

Combine the flaxseed with the warm water to make your flax egg then
set aside for 10 minutes to thicken.

In an electric stand mixer with a paddle attachment, combine the dry
ingredients.

In a separate bowl, combine the wet ingredients including the flax egg.
Then add the wet ingredients into the dry ingredients, and mix for 2
minutes to ensure they are well incorporated.

Divide the cake mixture evenly between each prepared tin. Place them
onto a baking tray. Bake for 30 minutes in the preheated oven until a
toothpick inserted into the centre of the cakes comes out clean. Leave
them to cool in the tin for 10 minutes before gently turning out onto a
wire rack to cool completely.

For the buttercream frosting
Drain and rinse the cashews, discarding the soaking water. Place
them into the blender with all the other ingredients and blitz until the
frosting is creamy and smooth.

Spread the frosting on top of the first cake, then place the second cake
on top like a sandwich and cover the top with the remaining frosting.

To finish
Decorate your cake with the walnut halves dotted around the edge and
orange zest liberally sprinkled over the top. Enjoy.

brownies

SERVES 8

I can't tell you how many times I've tweaked my brownie recipe over the years, to perfect the version below. At least a hundred, if not more. It's been absolutely worth it to create a brownie as good, if not better than my 2011 original. The chia provides the right amount of 'squidge' and the almonds make it more fudgy than cakey. It's the best of all brownie worlds.

For the chia-egg
1 tbsp chia seeds
3 tbsp warm water

Dry Ingredients
200g plain flour, sifted
50g ground almonds
300g coconut sugar
1 tsp bicarbonate of soda, sifted
60g cacao powder, sifted
Pinch of Himalayan salt

Wet Ingredients
100ml almond milk
130g coconut oil, melted

For the topping
2 tbsp chopped walnuts, pistachios, pecans or cacao nibs

Preheat the oven to 180°c and lightly grease a 20cm square or rectangular tin with melted coconut oil. Line the base with parchment paper.

Place the chia seeds in a bowl with the warm water, mix well then leave to one side for 10 minutes to thicken up. Stir once in this time to ensure the dry seeds on top have taken on the water below.

In an electric stand mixer with a paddle attachment, combine your dry ingredients. In a separate bowl, mix the almond milk and melted coconut oil with the chia-egg.

Add the wet ingredients to the dry ingredients and leave to mix well for around 5 minutes to ensure all the oil has been incorporated. You will be left with a shiny and very thick mixture.

Pour this into the lined tin and press it down firmly and evenly using a silicone spatula. Sprinkle the brownie with your topping of choice, then bake for 30 minutes in the preheated oven until cooked through but still a little soft in the middle. It will continue cooking from the residual heat of the tin once out the oven.

Leave the brownie to cool in the tin for 10 minutes, then carefully transfer it to a wire rack by lifting the paper. After another 10 minutes, carefully use another wire rack to turn it upside down and gently remove the paper. Leave to cool completely (this part is very important) before cutting into squares. Enjoy.

victoria sponge cake

SERVES 8

It's a tea-time winner and every bite is so light and delicious.
Quintessentially British and a far healthier version of the classic.

For the flax egg
1 tbsp ground flaxseed
3 tbsp warm water

Dry Ingredients
300g self-raising flour, sifted
140g coconut sugar
1 tsp bicarbonate of soda, sifted
1 tsp baking powder, sifted
1 tsp arrowroot, sifted
¼ tsp vanilla powder
½ tsp Himalayan salt

Wet Ingredients
290ml almond milk
165ml sunflower oil
¼ tsp white rice vinegar

For the filling
200g strawberry conserve (p.42)

For the vanilla whipped cream
400g good quality coconut yoghurt
2 tbsp maple syrup
½ tsp vanilla powder or paste
100g fresh strawberries, halved with the
green tops left on

For the cake

Preheat the oven to 180°c and lightly grease two 20cm sandwich tins with sunflower oil. Line the bases with parchment paper.

Combine the flaxseed with the warm water to make your flax egg and set aside for 10 minutes to thicken.

Mix all the dry ingredients with a paddle attachment in an electric stand mixer until well combined.

In a separate bowl, combine all the wet ingredients including the flax egg.

Slowly add the wet ingredients to the dry while mixing them together, then continue to mix for 2 minutes until the mixture is smooth.

Pour the cake mixture into the prepared tins, dividing it equally. Place them onto a baking tray and then bake for 20 minutes or until the cakes have no wobble in the centre and a toothpick comes out clean.

Leave them to cool in the tin for 10 minutes, and then gently turn them out onto a wire rack to cool.

For the filling

Once cool, gently spread your strawberry conserve on the top of the first cake, and then place the second cake on top.

For the vanilla whipped cream

Scoop your coconut yoghurt into a bowl and use an electric whisk to whip it until thick and doubled in size. Add the maple syrup and vanilla at the very end. Keep the 'whipped cream' in the fridge until required, then pipe it on top of the cake and finish with the fresh strawberries.

decadent chocolate cake

SERVES 8

This is such an amazingly rich and moist cake; it's fantastic for birthdays or just as an afternoon treat.

For the chocolate ganache

300g cacao paste

2 tbsp coconut sugar

300ml tinned coconut milk, shaken well before opening

For the cake

Wet Ingredients

350ml almond milk

1½ tsp apple cider vinegar

150ml sunflower oil

2 tsp vanilla extract or paste

Dry Ingredients

230g self-raising flour, sifted

85g cacao powder, sifted

1 tsp baking powder, sifted

1 tsp bicarbonate of soda, sifted

260g coconut sugar

¼ tsp Himalayan salt

For the decoration

Fresh raspberries

Preheat the oven to 180°c and lightly grease two 20cm sandwich tins with sunflower oil. Line the bases with parchment paper.

For the chocolate ganache

Make this first as it needs ample time to firm up before it can be used as a filling and topping. Chop up the cacao paste and place it in a heatproof bowl with the coconut sugar. In a saucepan, heat the coconut milk until just boiling, then pour it over the cacao paste and sugar and stir until all the chocolate has melted.

Set the ganache aside for 2 minutes, then stir again until completely smooth. Cover and place in the fridge to cool for a minimum of 2 hours. If it's too hard when you remove it later on, simply sit it in a bain-marie of warm water.

For the cake

Mix the almond milk and vinegar in a large bowl. Add in the oil and vanilla and stir well.

In a separate bowl, mix together the flour, cacao powder, baking powder and bicarbonate of soda, then stir in the coconut sugar and salt.

By hand or with a paddle attachment on an electric stand mixer, combine the wet ingredients with the dry ingredients until everything is well incorporated and you have a smooth batter.

Divide this evenly between the two prepared tins on a baking tray and bake for 30 minutes in the preheated oven, until a toothpick inserted into the centre comes out clean.

Leave the cakes to cool in their tins for 10 minutes, then carefully turn them out onto a wire rack to cool completely before decorating.

For the decoration

Spread half of the ganache over one of the cakes, then place the other cake on top. Spread the remaining ganache over the top of the cake, and finish with fresh raspberries dotted around the edge. Enjoy.

sticky toffee pudding

SERVES 6

After a roast dinner in winter time, this would always be a treat, yet all the butter, sugar and cream that goes into the decadent and delicious traditional pudding is just too much. Here is my healthier version which is just as moist and will surprise you. It's even more delicious served with a scoop of vanilla nice cream too (p.270).

For the pudding

110g coconut oil, plus extra for greasing
120ml water
200g Medjool dates, pitted
110g coconut sugar
200g self-raising flour, sifted
1 tsp bicarbonate of soda, sifted
240ml almond milk
4 tbsp maple syrup
1 tbsp apple cider vinegar

For the toffee sauce

400ml tinned coconut milk, shaken well
before opening
200g coconut sugar
¼ tsp Himalayan salt

For the pudding

Preheat the oven to 170°c and lightly grease a small heatproof lasagne or pie dish with coconut oil.

Add the water and dates to a small saucepan and simmer for 5 minutes, until the dates have absorbed at least half of the water, then use an immersion blender to whizz them into a purée.

In a small saucepan, melt the coconut oil and then pour it into a bowl with the coconut sugar and stir until all the sugar has been dissolved.

Stir the flour and bicarbonate of soda into the coconut oil and sugar mixture, then mix in the almond milk and maple syrup.

Lastly, stir in the date purée and apple cider vinegar. Mix until everything has been well incorporated and the batter is smooth.

Pour the mixture into the prepared dish and cover tightly with foil. Bake for 1 hour and 10 minutes, until a toothpick inserted into the middle of the pudding comes out clean.

For the toffee sauce

Add all your ingredients to a saucepan over a medium to high heat, stirring to combine everything while it comes to the boil and starts to thicken.

Remove the pan from the heat and pour the toffee sauce into a jug ready for serving. You can make this in advance and store it in the fridge, then gently reheat in a saucepan before serving, or make your toffee sauce while the pudding bakes. Pour it while hot over your servings of sticky toffee pudding.

Tarts & Cheesecakes

dulce de leche cheesecake

SERVES 8

This is decadent and every bite is simply heavenly. It doesn't last long at mymuybueno Deli or in my home freezer. Creamy vanilla cheesecake with sweet caramel, what's not to love? You can even make a salted caramel version by adding more salt to your dulce de leche.

For the base
70g macadamias

70g almonds

70g pecans

100g brown rice syrup or maple syrup

40g desiccated coconut

80g Medjool dates, pitted

¼ tsp vanilla powder

⅛ tsp Himalayan salt

For the filling
400g cashews, soaked in water overnight

120g brown rice syrup or maple syrup

6 tbsp carton coconut milk

¼ tsp vanilla powder

Pinch of Himalayan salt

100g cacao butter

For the dulce de leche
200g Medjool dates, pitted

3 tbsp brown rice syrup or maple syrup

2 tbsp almond butter

2 tbsp water

¼ tsp vanilla powder

Pinch of Himalayan salt

For the base
Line a 20cm cake tin with parchment paper. Place the macadamias, almonds and pecans into the food processor and whizz until they have broken down into small pieces. Add all the other ingredients and process until well blended and sticky. Press the base firmly and evenly into the prepared cake tin to ensure it's well compacted then freeze.

For the filling
Drain and rinse the cashews, discarding the soaking water, then blitz them in the processor with the syrup, coconut milk, vanilla and salt.

In a saucepan, melt your cacao butter until it becomes liquid. Add this to the processor last and continue to blend until the mixture is smooth and creamy.

Pour half of your vanilla cheesecake mixture over the set base in the tin, then tap the whole tin on a flat surface to remove any air bubbles and settle the mixture evenly.

For the dulce de leche
Put all of your ingredients into the food processor and blitz well until thick, creamy and smooth.

With a teaspoon, dollop blobs of the dulce de leche all over the filling, ensuring you also get some blobs right to the very edge. Run a toothpick through the blobs in S movements to distribute the caramel. You want to create a marble effect, but as the caramel is thick you also want good size blobs left, so that when you cut the cheesecake it will look great and you'll get a good bite of caramel when eating it.

Repeat this process with a second layer of the cheesecake filling and caramel until you have used them both up.

Place the cheesecake back into the freezer and leave overnight to completely firm up. Remove the cheesecake from the freezer at least 10 minutes before you wish to serve, allowing it ample time to thaw and become easy to cut.

salted caramel cake

SERVES 8

This is hugely popular at mymuybueno Deli and our best-selling raw dessert. It's really decadent, but totally guilt-free, and you can really feel the benefits of the nuts and dates as you eat it for a completely natural sweet fix. It's wonderful for a special occasion, or just to keep in your freezer to indulge with a slice whenever you wish. My boys absolutely love it.

For the base
80g cashews
80g macadamias
50g almonds
45g buckwheat
45g desiccated coconut
45g brown rice syrup or maple syrup
80g Medjool dates, pitted
Pinch of Himalayan salt

For the caramel centre
200g Medjool dates, pitted
60ml coconut oil, melted
110g almond butter
125g maple syrup
¼ tsp vanilla powder
⅛ tsp Himalayan salt

For the chocolate
60g cacao butter
40g cacao powder
50g maple syrup
¼ tsp flaked sea salt

For the base

Place the cashews, macadamias and almonds into the food processor then blitz into small pieces. Add the buckwheat, coconut, syrup, dates and salt then continue to process. The mixture will start to combine; when that happens transfer it into a round 20cm cake tin lined with parchment paper. Press the base evenly into the base of the tin and place in the freezer to firm up.

For the caramel centre

Blend the dates, coconut oil, almond butter, maple syrup, vanilla powder and salt in the food processor. The mixture needs to be completely smooth so continue blending until all the lumps have disappeared. Spread the caramel over the set base and put the tin back into the freezer while you make the chocolate.

For the chocolate

Melt the cacao butter in a saucepan over a very low heat. Ensure it has completely melted, then combine the cacao butter with the cacao powder and maple syrup in a bowl. Whisk until you have a glossy mixture. Be careful not to allow it to seize. If you are in a cold environment, you must be very quick at this stage.

Pour the chocolate over the caramel in the tin and push it around quickly with a silicone spatula to spread it well and leave swirls on the top. Place the cake into the freezer to set overnight.

Remove from the freezer at least 10 minutes before you wish to serve the cake, to allow it ample time to thaw and be easy to cut. Sprinkle the flaked sea salt on top before serving.

strawberries and cream

SERVES 12

Nothing beats the combination of strawberries and cream. If it's for a special occasion, I like to do an extra strawberry layer at the bottom with more powder added to create an ombre-style cake.

For the base

80g cashews

80g almonds

80g macadamias

45g buckwheat

80g desiccated coconut

100g brown rice syrup

120g Medjool dates, pitted

Pinch of Himalayan salt

For the filling: layer 1

300g cashews, soaked in water overnight

100g brown rice syrup or maple syrup

5 tbsp carton coconut milk

Pinch of Himalayan salt

100g cacao butter

4 tbsp strawberry powder

For the filling: layer 2

300g cashews, soaked in water overnight

100g brown rice syrup or maple syrup

5 tbsp carton coconut milk

100g cacao butter

½ tsp vanilla powder

For the topping

100g fresh strawberries, halved with the green tops left on

For the base

Line a 20cm cake tin with parchment paper. In the food processor, blend the cashews, almonds and macadamias into small pieces. Add all the other ingredients and process until well combined. Press the mixture firmly and evenly into the base of tin so it's well compacted and place in the freezer to set.

For the filling

You will be making this filling twice to create the two layers. Drain and rinse the cashews, discarding the soaking water, then put them in your blender with the syrup, coconut milk and salt.

In a saucepan, melt your cacao butter until it becomes liquid. Add this to the blender last and continue to blend until the mixture is smooth and creamy. This is your default cheesecake filling.

Add your four tablespoons of strawberry powder and blend well. Pour the cheesecake mixture onto the base to form your first layer of filling.

Tap the whole tin on the counter to release any air bubbles and help it evenly form the next layer. Place into the freezer. Wash up your blender in order to repeat the above step using the vanilla powder to make the second layer of filling.

Ensure your first layer is frozen well for at least an hour before adding the next layer. Tap the whole tin onto the counter to release any air bubbles and help it evenly form your vanilla layer. Place the completed cheesecake back into the freezer and leave overnight to completely firm up.

Remove the cheesecake from the freezer at least 10 minutes before you wish to serve, to allow it ample time to thaw and be easy to cut. Top with the fresh strawberries to serve.

pecan pie

SERVES 8

This is a decadent and delicious dessert, another best seller at mymuybueno Deli. I love it with vanilla whipped cream (p.236). The base is baked, but the filling is raw. You could omit the flour and make this a completely raw pie if you wish. Simply follow all the steps below but freeze the base instead of baking it.

For the base

100g almonds

50g pecans

150g plain flour, sifted

60g maple syrup

30g coconut oil, melted

2 tsp ground cinnamon

100g Medjool dates, pitted

Pinch of Himalayan salt

For the filling

150g pecans

250g almond butter

200g Medjool dates, pitted

60g maple syrup

¼ tsp ground nutmeg

¼ tsp vanilla powder

Pinch of Himalayan salt

60ml water

For the topping

200g pecans

60g maple syrup

1 tsp ground cinnamon

Preheat your oven to 180°c. Lightly grease a 20cm fluted loose-bottomed tart tin with coconut oil, then line the base with parchment paper.

For the base

Place the almonds and pecans into a food processor and blend for a minute until they have a flour-like consistency, then add the plain flour, maple syrup, coconut oil, cinnamon, dates and salt. Blend again to form a sticky mixture.

Press this firmly but gently into the prepared tart tin, so it forms your pastry-like base. Prick the base a few times with a fork and place the tin on a baking tray. Bake for 10 minutes or until golden brown. Remove it from the oven and leave in the tin for 10 minutes to cool, then gently turn the base out and leave it to cool completely on a wire rack.

For the filling

While the base is cooling, blitz the pecans in the food processor for a minute so they become a cross between nut butter and flour, then add the almond butter. Once those have mixed together well, add the dates, syrup, nutmeg, vanilla and salt. Allow these to blend well as you gradually add the water. The mixture should be smooth and free from lumps. Keep this in the fridge until needed.

For the topping

Place the pecans in a bowl with the maple syrup and cinnamon, give them a stir to coat the nuts, then spread them out on a baking tray, ensuring they are all turned upwards, and bake for 5 minutes at 180°c. Do not pour the excess liquid over them, otherwise they will all stick together in a pool of caramel. They should become a little browned and crunchy, but be careful they don't get too dark or catch. I love these on their own or to give as gifts because they're so good.

Fill the cooled pie base with your delicious pecan caramel, ensuring you carefully push it to all sides, and smooth it out with a silicone spatula. Press it down to get a smooth even surface.

Place your maple-glazed pecans on the top in a pattern, starting in the centre and spiralling outwards until all the pecans are used up.

Place the pecan pie into the freezer and leave overnight to completely firm up.

Remove it from the freezer 10 minutes before you wish to serve, to allow the pie ample time to thaw and be easy to cut.

raspberry jam cheesecake

SERVES 8

This is such a beautiful cheesecake, and it's fantastic with blueberries too, so do try making both flavours. The colour is vibrant and the taste of the lemon with the creamy sweet cheesecake and the sharpness of the berries is a perfect combination.

For the base

60g cashews

60g almonds

60g macadamias

45g buckwheat

45g desiccated coconut

45g brown rice syrup or maple syrup

100g Medjool dates, pitted

For the jam

2 tbsp chia seeds

6 tbsp warm water

250g raspberries

3 tbsp brown rice syrup or maple syrup

For the cheesecake

500g cashews, soaked in water overnight

50ml lemon juice

5 tbsp carton rice milk

100g brown rice syrup or maple syrup

Pinch of Himalayan salt

100g cacao butter

½ lemon, zested

For the base

Blitz the cashews, almonds and macadamias to small pieces in the food processor. Add the remaining ingredients and blend until everything is well combined and the mixture is sticky.

Press the mixture firmly and evenly, so it's well compacted, into a round 20cm cake tin lined with parchment paper. Place in the freezer so the base can firm up.

For the jam

Stir the chia seeds into the warm water in a small bowl and leave to thicken. Blend the raspberries in the food processor until smooth, then add the syrup and continue to process. Once the chia seed mixture has thickened, add the raspberry purée and stir well. Place the jam in the fridge to firm up.

For the cheesecake

Drain and rinse the cashews, discarding the soaking water, then place them into your blender with the lemon juice, rice milk, syrup and salt.

In a saucepan, melt your cacao butter until it becomes liquid. Add this to the blender last and continue to blend well until the mixture is smooth and creamy, then gently fold in the lemon zest.

Pour half of your cheesecake mixture over the set base in the tin, then tap the whole tin on a flat surface to remove any air bubbles and settle the mixture evenly.

Add dollops of your jam then swirl it through the cheesecake in S movements with a toothpick for a marble effect. There should still be large patches of jam for the visual effect when cutting a slice, and also the taste of the fruit when eating it.

Pour the remaining cheesecake mixture over the top, repeat the marbling effect with the jam and add final flecks of lemon zest to the top. Place the tin back into the freezer and leave overnight for the cheesecake to set completely.

Remove it from the freezer 10 minutes before you wish to serve the cheesecake, allowing it ample time to thaw slightly and be easy to cut.

chocolate orange cheesecake

SERVES 8

For all the chocolate orange lovers out there, you will absolutely adore this.

For the base

100g pecans

100g almonds

80g desiccated coconut

2 tbsp cacao powder

100g Medjool dates, pitted

1 tsp vanilla powder

Pinch of Himalayan salt

100g brown rice syrup or maple syrup

For the filling

400g cashews, soaked in water overnight

100g brown rice syrup or maple syrup

6 tbsp carton coconut milk

70g cacao powder

Pinch of Himalayan salt

100g cacao butter

100ml fresh orange juice

1 tsp orange extract

For the topping

1 orange

For the base

Line a 20cm cake tin with parchment paper. In the food processor, blend the pecans and almonds into small pieces. Add all the other ingredients and process until well combined and sticky. Press the mixture firmly and evenly into the base of the tin so it's well compacted and place in the freezer to firm up.

For the filling

Drain and rinse the cashews, discarding the soaking water, then blitz them in the processor with the syrup, coconut milk, cacao and salt.

In a saucepan, melt your cacao butter until it becomes liquid. Add this to the processor last and continue to blend until the mixture is smooth and creamy.

Add the orange juice and extract and then blend again until well incorporated.

Pour the filling over the base and tap the whole tin down on the counter firmly to release any air bubbles and help to distribute it evenly in the tin.

Place the cheesecake back into the freezer and leave overnight to completely firm up. Remove from the freezer at least 10 minutes before you wish to serve the cheesecake, allowing it ample time to thaw and be easy to cut.

For the topping

Before serving, zest the orange directly over the cheesecake so that the oils and juice release over the cake. Cover it generously, being careful not to include any white pith as this is bitter.

blueberry tart

SERVES 8

This is a real showstopper and one of my favourite desserts to bring when visiting friends for lunch; turning up with one of these is guaranteed to put a smile on everyone's face. It requires a little effort, but the finish is so very worth it. The base is cooked and the filling is raw.

For the base

150g jumbo rolled oats
50g ground almonds
25g desiccated coconut
50g maple syrup
50g coconut oil, melted
Pinch of Himalayan salt

For the filling

350g cashews, soaked in water overnight
100ml coconut oil, melted
100ml carton coconut milk
200ml water
250g brown rice syrup or maple syrup
Pinch of Himalayan salt
¼ tsp vanilla powder
2 tbsp lemon juice
3 tbsp blueberry powder
400g fresh blueberries, to decorate

Preheat your oven to 180°c. Lightly grease a 20cm fluted loose-bottomed tart tin with coconut oil, then line it with parchment paper.

For the base

Add the rolled oats to your food processor and whizz up to a flour-like texture. Add the remaining ingredients and blend until well combined.

Press the mixture into your prepared tart tin evenly and prick the base a few times with a fork, place onto a baking tray, then bake in the preheated oven for 10 minutes or until golden brown. Remove it from the oven and leave in the tin for 10 minutes to cool, then gently turn the base out and leave it to cool completely on a wire rack.

For the filling

While the base is cooling, drain and rinse the cashews, discarding the soaking water, then process them in a blender with the melted coconut oil, coconut milk, water, syrup and salt until smooth.

You now need to separate the mixture. Pour half of it into a jug and stir in the vanilla powder and lemon juice. Add the blueberry powder to the other half of the mixture, which is still in the blender, with an extra tablespoon of water and blend until smooth, then pour into another jug.

Holding both jugs, one in each hand, pour the filling mixtures over the cooled tart base, ensuring the vanilla and blueberry mixtures are layered and dolloped evenly. Swirl them together with a toothpick in S movements to get a beautiful marbled effect, but less is more, so try not to overdo this.

Place the tart in the freezer for 15 minutes, then as the cheesecake mixture starts to set you can add the fresh blueberries, pressing them very gently into the filling around the edge. Place the decorated tart back into the freezer and leave overnight to completely firm up.

Remove it from the freezer 10 minutes before you wish to serve the tart, allowing it ample time to thaw and become easy to cut.

celebration cheesecake

SERVES 12

This can be made with one flavoured filling for a simple cheesecake, or you can mix and match layers of vanilla, chocolate, blueberry, raspberry or matcha. As demonstrated in the recipe below, you can even do all five flavours for a special occasion; perfect for birthdays.

For the base
100g pecans
80g almonds
45g desiccated coconut
25g cacao powder
100g brown rice syrup or maple syrup
120g Medjool dates, pitted
Pinch of Himalayan salt

For the filling
300g cashews, soaked in water overnight
100g brown rice syrup or maple syrup
5 tbsp carton coconut milk
Pinch of Himalayan salt
100g cacao butter

For the vanilla layer
¼ tsp vanilla powder

For the chocolate layer
50g cacao powder

For the blueberry layer
100g fresh blueberries
or 2 tbsp blueberry powder

For the raspberry layer
100g fresh raspberries
or 2 tbsp raspberry powder

For the matcha layer
1 tsp matcha powder

For the chocolate glaze
100ml coconut oil, melted
60g cacao powder
50g maple syrup

To finish
Decorate with your choice of energy balls, fresh fruit, edible flowers, cacao nibs, coconut flakes

For the base

Line a 20cm cake tin with parchment paper. Process the pecans and almonds in a blender until they have broken down into small pieces. Add all other ingredients and process until well blended and sticky. Press the base into the prepared cake tin firmly and evenly so it is well compacted and freeze.

For the filling

Drain and rinse the cashews, discarding the soaking water, then blitz them in the processor with the syrup, coconut milk and salt. In a saucepan, melt your cacao butter until it becomes liquid. Add this to the processor last and continue to blend until the mixture is smooth and creamy.

This is your default cheesecake base. Repeat this process to make the rest of your fillings, simply adding the powders or fresh fruit to create each flavour. They may need an extra tablespoon of coconut milk as the powders will dry the mix out, but it won't be necessary if you are using fresh berries, as there will be enough extra liquid from them.

Pour the first layer into the tin over the set base, tap the whole tin onto the counter to release any air bubbles and help it to settle evenly, then ensure it has been frozen for at least an hour before adding the next layer. Place the finished cheesecake back into the freezer and leave overnight to completely firm up.

Remove the celebration cheesecake from the freezer 10 minutes before you wish to serve it, allowing it ample time to thaw and become easy to cut.

For the chocolate glaze

Simply whisk all the ingredients together in a bowl, then use the glaze immediately.

Decorate your creation only once you're ready to serve, while it's thawing. If you are using the chocolate glaze, drizzle it on while the cheesecake is still frozen, as it will firm up beautifully.

Nice Creams

choc-nices

MAKES 10

These mini nice creams are so yummy and my freezer is full of them. They take a little effort to make, but then you have them handy to enjoy on an afternoon or as a light after dinner treat. A throwback to a retro choc-ice.

For the nice cream

400ml tinned coconut milk, refrigerated overnight

150g cashews, soaked in water overnight

40g maple syrup

1 tsp vanilla powder or paste

Alternative flavours (if using, leave out the vanilla in the nice cream)

2 tsp cacao powder

1 tsp peppermint extract

1 tsp freeze-dried raspberry powder

1 tsp matcha powder

For the salted caramel (if using)

80ml tinned coconut milk, refrigerated overnight

120g Medjool dates, pitted

½ tsp vanilla powder or paste

$\frac{1}{8}$ tsp Himalayan salt

For the chocolate glaze

100ml coconut oil, melted

60g cacao powder

50g maple syrup

Toppings

Crushed almonds or pistachios

Desiccated coconut

Freeze-dried raspberries

Cacao nibs

For the nice cream

You will need mini silicone ice cream moulds for this recipe and mini wooden sticks.

Do not shake the tin of coconut milk, just remove it from the fridge, open and gently scrape the coconut cream off the top. Put this into your blender and discard the clear liquid. Drain and rinse the cashews, discarding the soaking water, then place them into the blender with all the other ingredients. Whizz everything together until you have a smooth mixture.

Place your moulds onto a baking tray and insert your wooden sticks. Pour the ice cream mixture into your moulds until they are three quarters full. Do not fill them up completely because you need to leave space for the caramel.

Alternatively, omit the caramel and add your preferred flavouring or simply use the vanilla nice cream as it comes, then fill the moulds to the top.

Place them into the freezer for 1 hour to firm up.

For the salted caramel (if using)

Do not shake the tin of coconut milk, just remove it from the fridge, open and gently scrape the coconut cream off the top. Put this into your food processor along with all your remaining ingredients and blend until creamy. Spread the caramel evenly into the remaining quarter of the moulds, then place them back into the freezer for 2 hours.

For the chocolate glaze

Whisk all the ingredients together in a bowl, then use the glaze immediately. Dip each nice cream into your chocolate glaze, sprinkle over your topping of choice, then place them on a baking sheet lined with parchment paper in the freezer until the chocolate shell has set.

Leave your choc-nice out for 5 minutes before eating so that the inside is creamy and not solid.

pistachio nice cream

When I worked on yachts, I was spoilt for choice with good quality gelato in Italy and I always opted for pistachio. It's my absolute favourite and making my own healthier version was something I was keen to master early on. Enjoy.

240g pistachios
400ml tinned coconut milk, refrigerated overnight
340ml carton almond milk
100g Medjool dates, pitted
4 tbsp maple syrup
1 tsp vanilla extract

Place the pistachios into your food processor and grind them into a flour, then put them into a blender. Do not shake the tin of coconut milk, just remove it from the fridge, open and gently scoop the thick coconut cream off the top. Discard the clear liquid. Place the coconut cream into your blender along with the almond milk, dates, syrup and vanilla.

Blend the mixture until completely smooth, then taste it and add more vanilla or syrup if needed.

Pour the mixture into your ice cream maker and leave to churn until ready. If you don't have an ice cream machine, you can skip this step and still achieve a good result. Pour into a large container and freeze.

Leave the pistachio nice cream to thaw for 10 minutes before serving so it has a creamy texture.

coconut nice cream

SERVES 6

This is so good on its own, and I love it with fresh pineapple for a light dessert. It also works brilliantly as an alternate filling for the choc-nices recipe on the previous page too.

800ml tinned coconut milk, refrigerated overnight
8 tbsp maple syrup
1 tsp vanilla powder or paste
Pinch of Himalayan salt

Shake one tin of coconut milk well and pour it into your blender., then just remove the other from the fridge without shaking it, open and gently scoop the coconut cream off the top. Add this to your blender and discard the clear liquid. Add the maple syrup, vanilla and salt and blend until well combined.

Pour the mixture into your ice cream maker and leave to churn until ready. If you don't have an ice cream machine, you can skip this step and still achieve a good result. Pour into a large container and freeze.

Leave the nice cream to thaw for 10 minutes before serving, so that it has a creamy texture.

vanilla nice cream

SERVES 6

Just like all vanilla ice cream, this is great on its own or with so many desserts, from my pecan pie
to sticky toffee pudding, and also Dorset apple cake.

800ml tinned coconut milk,
refrigerated overnight
250g cashews, soaked in water overnight
8 tbsp maple syrup
½ tsp vanilla powder

Shake one tin of coconut milk well and pour it into your blender, then just remove the other from the fridge without shaking it, open and gently scoop the coconut cream off the top. Add this to your blender and discard the clear liquid.

Drain and rinse the cashews, discarding the soaking water, then add them to your blender with the syrup and vanilla. Blend until smooth.

Pour the mixture into your ice cream maker and leave to churn until ready. If you don't have an ice cream machine, you can skip this step and still achieve a good result. Pour into a large container and freeze.

Leave the nice cream to thaw for 10 minutes before serving, so that it has a creamy texture.

quick chocolate or strawberry nice cream

SERVES 1

This is so fast and easy, a brilliant solution whenever my boys ask for ice cream and we are all out. I always
keep my freezer full of ripe bananas and within a few minutes it's in their hands being demolished.

2 frozen bananas, sliced
3 tbsp tinned coconut milk,
shaken well before opening
2 Medjool dates, pitted
¼ tsp vanilla powder
2 tbsp cacao powder
OR
80g fresh strawberries

Place the frozen bananas into a food processor and blend until smooth. Add the coconut milk, dates and vanilla powder along with your flavour of choice, then blend again until incorporated.

Enjoy your chocolate or strawberry nice cream straight away.

chocolate and peanut nice creams

MAKES 8

These are more to satisfy my own love of chocolate and peanut butter than for my boys, but of course they love them too. They are equally good with almond butter and crushed almonds if you aren't a peanut fan.

For the nice cream
400ml tinned coconut milk, refrigerated overnight
150g cashews, soaked in water overnight
4 tbsp peanut butter
¼ tsp vanilla powder
120g maple syrup
Pinch of Himalayan salt

For the peanut caramel
200g Medjool dates, pitted
2 tbsp coconut oil, melted
3 tbsp peanut butter
60ml water
Pinch of Himalayan salt

For the chocolate glaze
100ml coconut oil, melted
60g cacao powder
50g maple syrup

To finish
4 tbsp crushed peanuts
Pinch of Himalayan salt

You will need ice lolly moulds and wooden sticks for this recipe.

For the nice cream

Do not shake the tin of coconut milk, just remove it from the fridge, open and gently scrape the coconut cream off the top, setting aside two tablespoons for the caramel. Put the rest into your food processor and discard the clear liquid.

Drain and rinse the cashews, discarding the soaking water, then add them to your food processor along with the peanut butter, vanilla, syrup and salt. Blend well until smooth, then pour the mixture into moulds, add your wooden sticks and freeze for a minimum of 4 hours.

For the peanut caramel

Soak the dates in hot water to really soften them, then drain and transfer them to a food processor. Blend until a paste forms. Add the coconut oil, peanut butter, water, the two tablespoons of coconut cream and salt then blend until completely smooth.

For the chocolate glaze

Whisk all the ingredients together in a bowl. Use the glaze immediately when the nice cream has frozen. Remove the nice creams from the moulds and lay them out on a baking tray lined with parchment paper. You may need to run a hot cloth over the moulds to loosen the nice creams. Using a palette knife, spread caramel down one side of the nice cream, sprinkle with crushed peanuts and salt which should stick, and then coat the whole thing, using a spoon to liberally pour the glaze over.

Lay them back on the baking sheet and place them into the freezer to harden completely.

Leave the nice cream to thaw for 10 minutes before serving, so that the inside is creamy and not solid.

fruity summer lollies

These are so delicious, and you can add whichever fruit you like to change the colour and flavours. Try kiwi for green or blueberry for purple lollies. You can change the fruit juice too, using apple for lighter colours, and orange for darker. Beetroot is also fantastic. So colourful, so hydrating and a winner with children and adults alike, every time.

For the yellow layer
180ml fresh apple juice
80g pineapple, peeled and chopped
80g mango

For the red layer
180ml fresh apple juice
120g strawberries, hulled
60g mango

For the orange layer
180ml fresh orange juice
1 whole orange, peeled, deseeded and chopped
80g mango

You will need ice lolly moulds and wooden sticks for this recipe.

Add your apple juice to a blender with the pineapple and mango. Blend until smooth then pour the yellow mixture into your lolly moulds, filling them a third of the way up, and insert your wooden sticks now. Freeze for about half an hour to make your first layer.

Next, add your apple juice to the blender with the strawberries and mango. Blend until smooth then repeat the layering and freezing process to make your second layer.

Add your orange juice to the blender with the chopped orange and mango. Blend until smooth then repeat the layering and freezing process to make your third and final layer.

Leave the lollies to freeze overnight and set completely. Run a hot cloth over the moulds to loosen the lollies and help you get them out. Enjoy.

creamy milk lollies

These are very close to the flavour of a popular childhood lolly, especially the strawberry one. Creamy and delicious.

1 ripe banana
125ml tinned coconut milk, shaken well before opening
1 tbsp maple syrup

Flavourings
250g mango, peeled and chopped
250g strawberries, hulled and chopped
250g pineapple, peeled and chopped

You will need ice lolly moulds and wooden sticks for this recipe.

Place the banana, coconut milk and syrup into the blender with your fruit flavouring of choice. Blend until the mixture is completely smooth.

Pour the mixture into your lolly moulds, add the wooden sticks and freeze until the next day. Run a hot cloth over the outside of the moulds to help loosen the lollies, which should be completely solid. Enjoy.

Acknowledgements

I could never have imagined just how much work it would take to bring this book together.

It has been a real labour of love and I couldn't have done it without the support of my amazing family, and everyone who has played a part in its process.

I want to thank certain individuals, past and present, who have not only helped me with this book, but who have been significant in various moments throughout my life that have led me to this stage.

Firstly to Paul, my husband, who is my absolute rock. From the moment we married, it truly was the first day of the rest of my life. Your support, your belief in my vision, and your own invested hard work and efforts have all been amazing. You are my best friend and I love you so much.

My boys, Seth and Jacob, who support me in everything because we are 'all in' as a team and family. We have our crazy sleepovers at my office when my schedule is bananas, we cook together, we play together; everything I do, I do for both of you.

My Granny, the woman I will always aspire to be, and I hope to always make proud.

Lou, you believed in me so very much, and that belief made me believe more in myself. I will miss you always but am honoured to have been your friend.

Jana, I am so grateful for your brilliant assistance with all the testing and measuring and retesting along the way, and for coming over too.

My amazing mymuybueno team, who have all been incredibly patient and supportive knowing how much busier I have been while knee-deep in this book and still doing my normal job, juggling a hundred balls at the same time.

Moosey, you have been like the big sister I never had, and the biggest and bestest friend I could ever have asked for. Lisa and Mama Trav, you are both a big part of my heart, my journey and my family.

To the chefs who have believed in me and in mymuybueno, my vision with the chef platform and cookery school, and can see everything I am working towards – thank you.

Paula, for introducing me to real food. I can even remember my first bacon sandwich, which you took me for, at the café across the road. Sammy, you would never have known at the time how much working for you and your family inspired me. I fell in love with all the food I cooked for you, and that time ignited both my vision for mymuybueno and a further passion for good food.

Thank you to Phil and all at Meze for supporting me with the creative direction I wanted for this book, helping it encompass everything I want to share. Clare, for your amazing photography. Pernilla, for totally understanding what I wanted to achieve, and for capturing my day to day, and my family time together. Jennifer, for your brilliant eye and expertise. Zoe, for nailing it with the gorgeous props. Mikey and Jaysam, for being my amazing glam squad always. Vanessa, for all your amazing help. Anne, for your input, knowledge and being a sounding board throughout this process. Brigita, for all your wonderful design work.

Your collective experience, talent, expertise and input made our team really special, and has filled the pages of this book beautifully, breathing so much life into each and every one. Thank you.

And of course, thank you Lord. None of this would be possible and I would not be the person I am, or have made it through any of my experiences, without you. You have helped me to be the woman I stand tall as today.

Index

dill
scrambled eggs with smoked salmon 50, spinach and feta frittata 77, thai green salad 160

dried cranberries
granola 30, feta, cranberry and pistachio couscous 156, mediterranean quinoa salad 169

dried yeast
pizza 138, bread rolls 196

E

eggs
blueberry muffins 39, pancakes 49, scrambled eggs with smoked salmon 50, spinach and feta frittata 77, coconut panko prawns 82, courgette and feta fritters 94, chicken ramen 116, mayonnaise 190, soft boiled eggs 197

F

fennel seeds
samosas 92

feta
spinach and feta frittata 77, courgette and feta fritters 94, greek salad 153, feta, cranberry and pistachio couscous 156, butternut squash, feta and chorizo salad 167

figs
fresh fruit platter 47, fig, mozzarella and serrano salad 163

filo pastry
samosas 92

fish sauce
thai green chicken curry 98, massaman curry 104, chickpea and sweet potato curry 106, chicken and prawn laksa 118, two ways with beef fillet 124, thai salmon 134, chilli glazed salmon skewers 134, spicy green papaya salad 158, thai chilli jam 195, chilli tomato chutney 195

flaxseed
banana bread 40, ultra seedy bread 42, ginger loaf 225, chocolate doughnuts 226, carrot cake 230, victoria sponge cake 236,

G

galangal
thai green chicken curry 98, massaman curry 104, chicken and prawn laksa 118, thai salmon 134

garam masala
samosas 92, chicken tikka masala 100, chickpea and sweet potato curry 106, raita 191

garlic
baked beans 52, plain and beetroot hummus 72, prawn and chive gyoza 80, chicken satays 83, samosas 92, courgette and feta fritters 94, thai green chicken curry 98, chicken tikka masala 100, lentil dahl 103, massaman curry 104, chickpea and sweet potato curry 106, lamb stew 110, oxtail stew 113, carrot and coriander soup 115, chicken ramen 116, chicken and prawn laksa 118, pasta carbonara 122, two ways with beef fillet 124, prawns with chilli, ginger & garlic butter 126, slow cooked lamb shoulder 128, paella 130, two ways with roast chicken 133, thai salmon 134, pizza 138, three ways with chicken wings 143, whole baked sea bass 144, lentils with maple and cumin roasted carrots 150, spicy green papaya salad 158, thai green salad 160, roasted turmeric cauliflower 175, garlic green beans 175, potato mash 178, roasted broccoli, garlic, chilli & parmesan 180, roasted mediterranean veg 180, roast potatoes 181, miso black beans, mushrooms & spinach 182, soy and garlic broccoli and pak choi 182, french dressing 188, pomegranate dressing 189, caesar dressing 189, mayonnaise 190, vegan mayonnaise 190, raita 191, almond butter dipping sauce 191, gyoza dipping sauce 191, tomato pasta sauce 192, pesto 192, thai chilli jam 195, chilli tomato chutney 195

garlic powder
three ways with chicken wings 143, vegan caesar dressing 189, tomato ketchup 190, vegan parmesan 192, spice rub 193

gem lettuce
rainbow rolls 85, prawn caesar salad 154

ginger, fresh
wake up juice 63, beet-i-full juice 66, chicken satays 83, sushi 91, samosas 92, thai green chicken curry 98, chicken tikka masala 100, lentil dahl 103, massaman curry 104, chickpea and sweet potato curry 106, chicken ramen 116, chicken and prawn laksa 118, prawns with chilli, ginger & garlic butter 126, thai salmon 134, three ways with chicken wings 143, spicy green papaya salad 158, miso black beans, mushrooms & spinach 182, soy and garlic

broccoli and pak choi 182, raita 191, almond butter dipping sauce 191, gyoza dipping sauce 191, chilli tomato chutney 195, energy balls 202, ginger loaf 225, carrot cake 230

ginger, ground
spiced matcha latte 56, golden turmeric latte 59, roasted turmeric cauliflower 175, tamarind dipping sauce 193, energy balls 202, ginger loaf 225

grapes
fresh fruit platter 47

greek yoghurt
vanilla chia pudding 34, blueberry muffins 39, pancakes 49, flatbreads 72, caesar dressing 189, raita 191

green beans
paella 130, spicy green papaya salad 158, thai green salad 160, garlic green beans 175

gyoza wrappers
prawn and chive gyoza 80

H

hazelnut
nut butters 44, hazelnut chocolate spread 47

honey
granola 30, vanilla chia pudding 34, spiced matcha latte 56, reishi chai latte 59, chicken satays 83, two ways with roast chicken 133, pizza 138, three ways with chicken wings 143, fig, mozzarella and serrano salad 163, honey roasted carrots 172, roasted balsamic beetroot 178, miso aubergines 184, honey and lemon dressing 188

horseradish
two ways with beef fillet 124

J

jasmine rice
plain rice 197, coconut rice 197

jumbo rolled oats
granola 30, overnight oats 34, banana bread 40, ultra seedy bread 42, energy balls 202, chocolate caramel biscuit bars 209, chia cinnamon doughnuts 214, vanilla doughnuts 217, oat cookies 228, blueberry tart 260

nutmeg, ground
hot chocolate 56, pomegranate dressing 189, energy balls 203, pecan pie 251

nutmeg, whole
smoothies 61, massaman curry 104, carrot and coriander soup 115, carrot cake 230

nutritional yeast
vegan caesar dressing 189, vegan carbonara sauce 192, vegan parmesan 192

O

olive oil
ultra seedy bread 42, avocado smash on toast 52, flatbreads 72, plain and beetroot hummus 72, guacamole 75, lamb stew 110, pasta carbonara 122, two ways with beef fillet 124, slow cooked lamb shoulder 128, pesto and parmesan salmon 136, pizza 138, whole baked sea bass 144, lentils with maple and cumin roasted carrots 150, greek salad 153, prawn caesar salad 154, feta, cranberry and pistachio couscous 156, butternut squash, feta and chorizo salad 167, mediterranean quinoa salad 169, honey roasted carrots 172, asparagus and parmesan 172, roasted turmeric cauliflower 175, roasted cherry tomatoes 175, garlic green beans 175, roasted balsamic beetroot 178, roasted broccoli, garlic, chilli & parmesan 180, roasted mediterranean veg 180, maple roasted sweet potato wedges 181, roast potatoes 181, french dressing 188, honey and lemon dressing 188, pomegranate dressing 189, caesar dressing 189, raita 191, tomato pasta sauce 192, pesto 192, bread rolls 196

olives
greek salad 153, mediterranean quinoa salad 169

onion
baked beans 52, guacamole 75, spinach and feta frittata 77, samosas 92, courgette and feta fritters 94, chicken tikka masala 100, lentil dahl 103, massaman curry 104, chickpea and sweet potato curry 106, lamb stew 110, oxtail stew 113, carrot and coriander soup 115, leek and potato soup 115, pasta carbonara 122, slow cooked lamb shoulder 128, paella 130, whole baked sea bass 144, tomato and pomegranate salad 148, lentils with maple and cumin roasted carrots 150, coleslaw 153, greek salad 153, roasted mediterranean veg 180, tomato pasta sauce 192, gravy 193

onion powder
three ways with chicken wings 143, tomato ketchup 190, spice rub 193

oranges
carrot cake 230, chocolate orange cheesecake 256, fruity summer lollies 274

oregano, dried
pizza 138

P

pak choi
chicken ramen 116, thai green salad 160, soy and garlic broccoli and pak choi 182

palm sugar
thai green chicken curry 98, massaman curry 104, chicken and prawn laksa 118, thai salmon 134, spicy green papaya salad 158, tamarind dressing 189, thai chilli jam 195, pineapple chutney 195, chilli tomato chutney 195

panko breadcrumbs
coconut panko prawns 82

paprika
baked beans 52, chicken tikka masala 100, chickpea and sweet potato curry 106, paella 130, three ways with chicken wings 143, roasted turmeric cauliflower 175, spice rub 193

parmesan
courgette and feta fritters 94, pasta carbonara 122, pesto and parmesan salmon 136, asparagus and parmesan 172, roasted broccoli, garlic, chilli & parmesan 180, caesar dressing 189, vegan parmesan 192, pesto 192

parsley, dried
three ways with chicken wings 143, spice rub 193

parsley, fresh
lamb stew 110, oxtail stew 113, pasta carbonara 122, prawns with chilli, ginger & garlic butter 126, paella 130, two ways with roast chicken 133, coleslaw 153, prawn caesar salad 154, feta, cranberry and pistachio couscous 156, mediterranean quinoa salad 169

passata
baked beans 52

passion fruit
fresh fruit platter 47

peaches
fresh fruit platter 47

peanut butter
overnight oats 34, chicken satays 83, satay sauce 191, energy balls 203, chocolate chip cookies 228, chocolate and peanut nice creams 272

peanuts
nut butters 44, chicken satays 83, massaman curry 104, spicy green papaya salad 158, energy balls 203, chocolate and peanut nice creams 272

peas
samosas 92, paella 130

pecans
maple, pecan and banana muffins 39, nut butters 44, energy balls 203, billionaire's shortbread 206, mint chocolate squares 210, brownies 235, dulce de leche cheesecake 244, pecan pie 251, chocolate orange cheesecake 256, celebration cheesecake 263

peppermint extract
mint chocolate squares 210, choc-nices 266

pickled ginger
sushi 91

pineapple
fresh fruit platter 47, green juice 63, beet-i-full juice 66, pineapple chutney 195, fruity summer lollies 274, creamy milk lollies 274

pine nuts
pesto 192

pistachios
nut butters 44, feta, cranberry and pistachio couscous 156, energy balls 203, brownies 235, choc-nices 266, pistachio nice cream 269

pomegranate
tomato and pomegranate salad 148

pomegranate molasses
pomegranate dressing 189

potatoes
samosas 92, massaman curry 104, leek and potato soup 115, potato mash 178, roast potatoes 181

prawns
prawn and chive gyoza 80, coconut panko prawns 82, rainbow rolls 85, chicken and prawn laksa 118, prawns with chilli, ginger & garlic butter 126, paella 130, prawn caesar salad 154,

psyllium husk
ultra seedy bread 42, chia cinnamon doughnuts 214, vanilla doughnuts 217